SCHOPENHAUER:
A GUIDE FOR THE PERPLEXED

Continuum *Guides for the Perplexed*

Continuum's Guides for the Perplexed are clear, concise and accessible introductions to thinkers, writers and subjects that students and readers can find especially challenging. Concentrating specifically on what it is that makes the subject difficult to grasp, these books explain and explore key themes and ideas, guiding the reader towards a thorough understanding of demanding material.

Guides for the Perplexed **available from Continuum:**

Adorno: A Guide for the Perplexed, Alex Thomson
Arendt: A Guide for the Perplexed, Karin Fry
Aristotle: A Guide for the Perplexed, John Vella
Augustine: A Guide for the Perplexed, James Wetzel
Bentham: A Guide for the Perplexed, Philip Schofield
Berkley: A Guide for the Perplexed, Talia Bettcher
Deleuze: A Guide for the Perplexed, Claire Colebrook
Derrida: A Guide for the Perplexed, Julian Wolfreys
Descartes: A Guide for the Perplexed, Justin Skirry
The Empiricists: A Guide for the Perplexed, Laurence Carlin
Existentialism: A Guide for the Perplexed, Stephen Earnshaw
Freud: A Guide for the Perplexed, Celine Surprenant
Gadamer: A Guide for the Perplexed, Chris Lawn
Habermas: A Guide for the Perplexed, Lasse Thomassen
Hegel: A Guide for the Perplexed, David James
Heidegger: A Guide for the Perplexed, David Cerbone
Hobbes: A Guide for the Perplexed, Stephen J. Finn
Hume: A Guide for the Perplexed, Angela Coventry
Husserl: A Guide for the Perplexed, Matheson Russell
Kant: A Guide for the Perplexed, TK Seung
Kierkegaard: A Guide for the Perplexed, Clare Carlisle
Leibniz: A Guide for the Perplexed, Franklin Perkins
Levinas: A Guide for the Perplexed, B. C. Hutchens
Locke: A Guide for the Perplexed, Patricia Sheridan
Merleau-Ponty: A Guide for the Perplexed, Eric Matthews
Nietzsche: A Guide for the Perplexed, R. Kevin Hill
Plato: A Guide for the Perplexed, Gerald A. Press
Pragmatism: A Guide for the Perplexed, Robert B. Talisse and Scott F. Aikin
Quine: A Guide for the Perplexed, Gary Kemp
Relativism: A Guide for the Perplexed, Timothy Mosteller
Ricoeur: A Guide for the Perplexed, David Pellauer
Rousseau: A Guide for the Perplexed, Matthew Simpson
Sartre: A Guide for the Perplexed, Gary Cox
Socrates: A Guide for the Perplexed, Sara Ahbel-Rappe
Spinoza: A Guide for the Perplexed, Charles Jarrett
The Stoics: A Guide for the Perplexed, M. Andrew Holowchak
Utilitarianism: A Guide for the Perplexed: Krister Bykvist

SCHOPENHAUER:
A GUIDE FOR THE PERPLEXED

R. RAJ SINGH

continuum

Continuum International Publishing Group
The Tower Building   80 Maiden Lane
11 York Road   Suite 704
London SE1 7NX   New York, NY 10038

www.continuumbooks.com

British Library Cataloguing-in-Publication Data
A catalogue record for this book is available from the British Library.

ISBN: HB: 978-0-8264-9141-1
       PB: 978-0-8264-9142-8

Library of Congress Cataloguing-in-Publication Data
Singh, R. Raj
Schopenhauer : a guide for the perplexed / R. Raj Singh.
p. cm.
Includes bibliographical references (p.) and index.
ISBN: 978-0-8264-9141-1
ISBN: 978-0-8264-9142-8
1. Schopenhauer, Arthur, 1788–1860. I. Title.
B3148.S54 2010
193–dc22
2009044989

Typeset by Newgen Imaging Systems Pvt Ltd, Chennai, India
Printed and bound in Great Britain by the MPG Books Group

To my esteemed teacher

John R. A. Mayer

CONTENTS

ACKNOWLEDGEMENTS

I wish to express my gratitude to Irene Cherrington, Administrative Assistant, Department of Philosophy, Brock University, for her substantive help in the preparation of this manuscript. I also want to thank my friend Louis Chenard for help with the proofs. I gratefully acknowledge Dover Publications, Inc. for permitting me to quote excerpts totalling 2409 words from the Dover edition (1966) of *The World as Will and Representation*, volumes I and II.

ABBREVIATIONS

Schopenhauer's works (with years of original publication):

BM   *On the Basis of Morality* (1840)
FRPSR *The Fourfold Root of the Principle of Sufficient Reason* (1813)
FW   *On the Freedom of Human Will* (1839)
PP   *Parerga and Paralipomena* (1851)
PP-I   *Parerga and Paralipomena*, vol. I
PP-II   *Parerga and Paralipomena*, vol. II
MR   *Manuscript Remains* in 4 volumes (1970)
WN   *On the Will in Nature* (1854)
WWR   *The World as Will and Representation* (1818)
W-I   *The World as Will and Representation*, vol. I (1818)
W-II   *The World as Will and Representation*, vol. II (1844)

INTRODUCTION

Schopenhauer is known for his brilliant writing style as well as for being a unique thinker. Generations of general readers and scholars have found his ideas stimulating and insightful and have found his writings delightfully easy to read in original and in translations. Schopenhauer's attractive writing style is free of the usual conceptual web spinnings and hair splitting arguments for which other philosophers, especially European philosophers are notorious. However, the readable nature of Schopenhauer's work does not diminish either his original contribution to philosophy, or the need for continuing assessment and interpretations of his philosophical system and of his various enigmatic concepts. Just as the work of other great philosophers like Plato, Descartes, Hume and Nietzsche is easy to read at first sight, but requires a great deal of analysis and interpretation, Schopenhauer's work too can be quite perplexing from a philosophical point of view.

The range of Schopenhauer's philosophical inquiry includes insights from religious thought; Christian ethics and Christian mysticism were his favourite sources. It also includes insights from the classical masters facilitated by Schopenhauer's vast knowledge of Greek and Latin sources. He often explores the thought contained in literatures of modern European languages and refers to writers like Goethe, Baltasar Gracián and Calderón. The fact that Schopenhauer treats Western and Eastern philosophies as one body of knowledge, and shows a deep appreciation of the thought systems of Hinduism and Buddhism, shows a cross-cultural approach in his philosophical methodology which was way ahead of his times. The fact that Schopenhauer led a fascinating life, which has been the object of numerous biographies, combined with the fact that his philosophy is so intertwined with the problems of living and being with others, makes him and his enigmatic thought ever so challenging for an interpreter. Besides all these special features of his philosophy, his connections with the work of past philosophers, especially with Plato and Kant by whom his system is deeply influenced, need to be assessed. The originality of Schopenhauer's ideas is validated by the fact that he had a considerable influence on several European and English philosophers and writers such as Nietzsche, Wagner, Tolstoy, Turgenev, Freud, Proust, Thomas Hardy, Thomas Mann, Wittgenstein and many others. That Schopenhauer was one of the few pessimistic thinkers with a heroic resolve to encounter the darker truths of life makes his thought not only uniquely fascinating but also a challenge for an interpreter.

For all these reasons, a serious reader cannot merely read Schopenhauer's primary works and form a judgement based on first impressions. Thus secondary literature has a role to play in offering assessments and interpretations of his uniquely built system, which rests on a single thought, namely, of the will-to-live which, according to him, is the core being of all things including all humanity. Many of Schopenhauer's other concepts that revolve around the focal point of the will are equally perplexing for a student interested in his philosophy. The general reader of his primary works without a background in the history of philosophy will also be baffled by Schopenhauer's assertions and will be prone to making simplistic judgements especially about this thinker's pessimism.

This book aims to offer Schopenhauer without tears to students as well as general readers, while offering to an advanced student, in many ways an original interpretation of Schopenhauer's thought along with the author's own critical assessments. Since Schopenhauer expressed the gist of his system in his chief work *The World as Will and Representation*, and in all of his subsequent works merely supplemented and explicated the substance of the same world-view, in this book we have chosen to focus primarily on *WWR* and secondarily on this thinker's other important works. All in all, in this Guide for the Perplexed an effort has been made to let the primary texts speak in their own voice. We have refrained from alluding to and evaluating the voluminous secondary literature, except for a few very important references in some of the chapters. A unique feature of this book is that it will provide a considerable analysis of Schopenhauer's Eastern sources, and will explicate the philosopher's own interpretations of the various standpoints of Vedanta and Buddhism. Unlike any other survey of Schopenhauer's entire philosophy, this book will outline how he fuses some of these Eastern concepts into his own system and stakes the claim of being one of the first trans-cultural thinkers in the West. But this guide for the perplexed does not highlight Schopenhauer's debt to Eastern thought at the cost of missing out on his connections with his own Western philosophical heritage. The influence of Platonic and Kantian thought and that of other figures of the history of Western philosophy on Schopenhauer's system is equally exposed.

In the first chapter, the life of Schopenhauer is resketched to provide important information about his unique, somewhat sad but colourful sojourn on this earth. It focuses on his intellectual journey, his writings and attempts to resolve several undue harsh critiques from Schopenhauer's other biographers, without ignoring some of the obvious character flaws of the great pessimist. Chapter Two exposes Schopenhauer's thesis that the world is primarily composed of the representations of the subject and his viewpoints on human perception, reason and knowledge. It also provides a summary of his very important previous work on the principle of sufficient reason, which Schopenhauer prescribes as essential reading for the understanding of his system. Chapter Three explores Schopenhauer's emphatic assertion that a dynamic force abides in all existents and this should be called the 'will'. The basic features of this all important concept in Schopenhauer's thought are initially described in *WWR*, but are referred to in all of his other writings. In Chapter Four, the aspects of suffering and the vanity of human life as described by this pessimistic philosopher are fully examined, and the pre-suppositions and important influences of Eastern ideas on this issue are exposed. The realistic nature of Schopenhauer's scathing critiques of human selfishness and apathy towards the weal and woe of others is outlined here. Chapter Five exposes Schopenhauer's theories of aesthetics and of the various art-forms such as architecture, painting, drama and music. His original philosophy of art to which he devotes approximately a quarter of his writings is analysed in this chapter.

Chapter Six explicates Schopenhauer's philosophical treatment of romantic love between the sexes, an issue that seldom received the attention of other philosophers. Many nuances of this fascinating subject-matter are herein exposed. In Chapter Seven, Schopenhauer's general connection with Eastern thought, especially with Vedanta and Buddhism is fully discussed. His interpretation of some Eastern concepts is critically evaluated. Many misunderstandings pertaining to his own major concepts such as those of suffering, moral undesirability of the world and eternal justice, caused by misunderstandings and non-recognition of his Eastern sources are also exposed. In Chapter Eight his reinterpretation of the standard ethical concepts from the vantage point of the will is fully explained. Chapter Nine exposes Schopenhauer's standpoints on Death, and its connection with philosophy as such, along with his ideas on any possible afterlife for the human entity. His status as a contemplator of death in the Socratean tradition is explained along with the fact that the theme of death is alive at every juncture of his thought. Chapter Ten discusses Schopenhauer's view that a denial of will is the summit of a higher ethical life and a unique possibility of human existence. It is explicated here that according to Schopenhauer, asceticism is invariably produced by a life of will's denial, and salvation must be an ultimate issue not just for the religions but also for any authentic philosophy.

CHAPTER ONE

A CONTEMPLATIVE LIFE

It is both fascinating and important to study an account of Schopenhauer's life. The biographies of most Western philosophers are given a cursory attention for their work is deemed to have little to do with their life-styles and/or the problems of living as such. Martin Heidegger fulfilled the requirement of providing a biographical sketch at the outset of one of his essays on Aristotle with the following cryptic statement: 'Aristotle was born, he worked and he died.' In case of Schopenhauer, however, his biographies provide important clues to his philosophy, and the harsh critiques of his biographers of his life-style, habits and his pessimistic outlook are indicative of the fact that his was a singular and colourful, but much misunderstood life. His philosophy is unique in being a study of the everyday life of the human entity and aims to delineate the possibilities of a life and salvation that is free of religious dogmas and superstition. He offers a comprehensive description of the miseries and trepidations of the everyday life of the human animal and suggests a way out in the form of a denial of the mundane pursuits and cravings. It is interesting therefore to look at the story of his own struggles to reconcile his sad, lonely but determined life with his philosophy. As one who believed so much in the connection between philosophy and living, he did not fail to show a lived philosophy in his own life. That his life and philosophy are both blamed too harshly for their pessimism often serves to hide his original insights and his determined, dauntless and compassionate life is another matter that we will try to outline. Of course, alongside his intellectual and moral merits not withstanding, he was not without numerous eccentricities, prejudices and egotistical traits. All this makes his life uniquely interesting and colourful.

In English language, two classical biographies of Schopenhauer by Helen Zimmern (1876) and by W. Wallace (1890) are available which are based on original biographies and collections of letters in German by W. Gwinner and J. Frauenstädt, two of the closest associates of Schopenhauer in the last phase of his life. A more recent intellectual biography authored by Rüdiger Safranski (1987) is also available in English translation by Edward Osars (1989). Many other biographies have been authored in German, English and French. One by A. Hübscher (1952) is most noteworthy. While the abovementioned works are all well-balanced and comprehensive, there are many others in secondary literature, which are unduly harsh in caricaturing Schopenhauer's life by focusing on his abnormalities and his negative and pessimistic approaches to human life. Many of his biographers, having scanty knowledge of Eastern philosophies, do not seem to sympathize with some of Schopenhauer's concepts inspired by Eastern thought which he blends with classical Western, especially Kantian and Platonic sources.

PARENTAGE, CHILDHOOD AND SCHOOL YEARS

Arthur Schopenhauer was born on 22 February 1788 in Danzig. Both his parents were of Dutch lineage but their ancestors for several generations had lived and flourished in the free city of Danzig being involved in primarily mercantile activities and secondarily as landlords and municipal politicians. The city of Danzig (currently, the Polish city of Gdansk) having been a member of the Hanseatic league of autonomous German mercantile towns was virtually a state by itself, although theoretically a part of the Polish kingdom. When Arthur was five years old, the city was annexed by Prussia and the family moved to Hamburg, another mercantile city state which was bigger, more stable and more autonomous than Danzig. Arthur's father, Heinrich Schopenhauer, was a successful businessman. He had travelled to England and France to gain first hand knowledge of the world and practical affairs. He was fluent in English and French besides his native German and was in the habit of reading foreign newspapers especially *The Times*. His house had a rich library and was full of mementos from his travels and tastefully decorated with specimens and works of art. It is curious that while he contemplated a business vocation for Arthur, he emphasized lived experience in foreign lands, especially in England and France as the most important part of his young son's education. He carefully named his son 'Arthur' for this name sounds equally native in English, French and German. Heinrich Schopenhauer was a short and stocky man of very impressive personality. He was hard of hearing from his early days and was prone to fits of depression and excessive anxiety throughout his life. In his last years, frequent bouts of rage also tainted his otherwise powerful character and record of accomplishments. It is interesting that Arthur inherited to a great extent his father's looks and personality traits, including a keen sense of money management. He was able to not only live on the wealth inherited from his father for his entire life as an independent scholar but also added on to it by wise investments, whereas his mother spent all of her resources and lived in straitened circumstances in her last years.

Arthur's mother, Johanna, also hailed from an influential family of Danzig. Married at age 18 to a man 20 years older than she, Johanna found new opportunities and leisure for her intellectual development. Heinrich's house was well-endowed for intellectual stimulus and her husband encouraged her literary apprenticeships. She was a good-looking woman of small and delicate frame with blue eyes and brown hair. Her husband could be proud of her cultivated intellect and sociable outlook. The couple was very fond of travelling and young Arthur always accompanied his parents. Wherever they went in Europe and England they found refined and celebrated company. Heinrich's plan of having his first child born in England was thwarted due to his wife's sudden illness, and upon their hasty return home the baby philosopher was born in Danzig. Arthur's first five years were spent in his native city being a darling of his youthful mother, who passed most of her time in the country house of the Schopenhauers on the outskirts of Danzig. The boy had some animals as his playmates and this early contact with animals may be responsible for his life-long empathy with non-human creatures.

Heinrich Schopenhauer was anxious about the takeover of his native city by the Prussian regime and was firmly resolved to flee from Danzig in case his fears materialized. In 1789 he did exactly that without caring for the disruption of his business and financial loss. The family of three moved to Hamburg, another mercantile Hanseatic city, confidently maintaining its free statehood. Arthur's childhood and early youth was spent in this vibrant European centre of trade, art and culture. The father's insistence that his son receives a cosmopolitan education combined with a first hand study of the world and things proved to be an asset for young Schopenhauer as he developed a preference for the study of real life and human nature rather than opting for abstractions and bookish knowledge. Soon after the birth of his only sister, Adele, at age 9 he accompanied his parents on a visit to France where his father left him under the guardianship of M. Gregoire for the next two years. He was treated very affectionately in the Gregoire household where he acquired fluency in the French language and became friends with M. Gregoire's son, Anthime, a friendship that would last for many years. Upon his return from France, Arthur was enrolled in a high school, where his father expected him to acquire education suitable for becoming a businessman.

At this time, Schopenhauer had begun to show preference for classics and philosophy and entreated his father to let him study these human sciences in a Gymnasium to prepare for a university education. But his father was not a man to be trifled with. He definitely aspired for a merchant's career for his son. Heinrich came up with an ingenious plan to nudge his son on to a business profession. He offered young Schopenhauer one of the two options, either to accompany his parents on a long voyage through Europe and England including a chance to revisit his friend Anthime in France, or to enter a Gymnasium to study philosophy and classics. The option to travel stipulated entrance into an apprenticeship with a senior merchant to gain experience for a business career. Schopenhauer, being a lad of 15 years, could not resist the temptation to travel and revisit his friend in France. The two-year-long travel took the Schopenhauer family to Holland, England, Scotland, France, Austria, etc. In England, Arthur was placed in a boarding house under the charge of Rev. Lancaster in the city of Wimbledon for three months, an experience that Arthur did not cherish. He despised the English boarding school system, religious dogmatism and hypocrisy of the higher classes. In his diary, which his mother encouraged him to keep for his travel records, young Schopenhauer already showed his tendency to keenly observe the instances of human misery and pitiable condition of the disadvantaged classes, the prisoners, the child labourers and the poor. Upon his return to Hamburg, Schopenhauer became an apprentice clerk in Herr Jenisch's merchant house in accordance with the pact he had made with his father.

Within a few months of joining the merchant house Schopenhauer suffered the loss of his father. The calamity was too much for him to bear. Heinrich went through a period of business downturn, had grown deaf and had shown signs of anxiety, depression and irritability. One day he fell from the balcony of his warehouse into a canal and was brought out dead. Whether it was a case of suicide or not, posterity will never know. Schopenhauer who respected and worshipped his father was heartbroken at this sudden turn of events. Although he carried on for two more years as the merchant's apprentice out of regard for the departed soul, his heart was not in the business career and he longed to be a scholar of classics and philosophy. Finally, at the urgings of his mother, and her friend Farnow, he began his studies in earnest at a school in Gotha and took additional tutorials in Greek and Latin. His studies at the Gymnasium at Gotha ended abruptly after six months due to a misadventure of caricaturing a schoolmaster which earned him the displeasure of his teachers. Arthur then moved to Weimar to continue his studies privately to enter a university and to stay with his mother briefly.

Schopenhauer applied himself rigorously to classical learning as well as mathematics, history and other subjects to prepare himself for entering a university. After annoying his mother, who could no longer bear living with him, he stayed in Weimar in his own lodgings for about two years. His flair for classical and modern languages and for the love of learning was quite evident by now.

SCHOPENHAUER'S UNIVERSITY DAYS

At age 21, Schopenhauer found himself financially well-provided thanks to the inheritance left by his father. He could also appreciate the wisdom of this parent, for it seemed that Heinrich had foreseen that his son having the scholarly inclinations would scarcely be able to succeed as a businessman and a man of the world. As is evident from a dedication that he composed to pay tribute to his father which was meant to be placed at the outset of his collected works, Arthur always worshipped the memory of his departed parent and benefactor with gratitude. He had quite the opposite feelings towards his surviving parent, whose life-style he did not approve of and considered her a bad influence on his young sister. He was afraid that his mother's spending habits would soon leave her and young Adele penniless. A few years later, while Arthur not only held on but added to his inherited funds, the mother lost most of her share due to unwise investments and frivolous spending. Schopenhauer's mistrust and dislike of his mother whom he never visited for the last 24 years of her life, and his disappointment about the timid nature of his sister, seem to be the factors in Schopenhauer's extreme views about women in general as expressed in his notorious essay 'On Women' in *Parerga and Paralipomena*, Vol. II. However, that he did not deny full personhood to all women and did have high estimation and regard for some female deniers of the will-to-live is evident from his tributes to Madame de Guyon, 'that great and beautiful soul, whose remembrance always fills me with reverence' and to the life of Fraulein Klettenberg composed by Goethe (W-I, 385).

In 1809, at age 21, Schopenhauer began his studies at the University of Göttingen enrolling himself in the medical faculty, which shows his deep interest in physical sciences and biology. In the first year he attended lectures on History, Geology, Physics, Botany, etc. In the second year, he shifted to the study of philosophy, but continued to sit in lectures on Astronomy, Ethnology and Physiology. His choices indicate his life-long interest in concrete and material reality of the phenomena of the world and his attempts to keep his philosophy untrammelled by mere abstractions. Deeply interested in all aspects of existence and mundane appearances of things, he may be regarded as a precursor of existentialism. Schopenhauer took copious notes and recorded his impressions of and responses to all the lecturers he heard. These manuscript books show us how hard he was on the scholars whose viewpoints he disliked or regarded as trivial. However, he had high regard for Schulze who advised him to begin his philosophical studies with Plato and Kant. While at Göttingen, Schopenhauer led the life of a meticulously dressed gentleman, with cultivated interests in music, especially flute playing, theatre, museums and in a careful study of nature. Although he was a reclusive, contemplative and highly independent young man, he did have friendly relations with some college mates. He was already known for his strong opinions and his excessively harsh critiques of professors, scholars and writers he did not approve of. In his writing as well he was prone to using strong expressions to castigate contemporary philosophers and writers whom he disliked, a regrettable habit that stayed with him all through life. Although his writing style was simple and lucid without pedantry and jargon, his contempt for opposing viewpoints comes through too strongly, turning his critiques into unseemly attacks on his intellectual rivals. His later-day attacks on Hegel also displayed immoderation and lack of refinement.

In 1811, Schopenhauer moved to University of Berlin drawn there for the prospect of attending Fichte's lectures. He continued his studies in natural sciences as well as hearing lectures on botany, anatomy, physics, chemistry, etc. He attended the lectures of Schleiermacher, Wolf and Fichte, some of the foremost philosophical luminaries of the day. His extensive note-books show that he took his studies seriously. They also show his excessive self-confidence and pride in his own philosophical abilities. He often dismissed the work of his teachers through critiques that deployed very strong words with gibes such as 'non-sense', 'sophist', 'twaddle', etc. he was disappointed with both Fichte and Schleiermacher. He felt that Fichte had departed objectionably from Kant's system and Schleiermacher unduly mixed philosophy with religion and theology. Wolf's lectures on Greek history and philology particularly attracted Schopenhauer. He greatly admired Wolf's original theories on classical Greek thought and history which were intellectually stimulating for him.

Schopenhauer did not suffer from the usual fault of national pride. He was not overly patriotic like many of his fellow academics. He wanted no interruptions to his scholarly quests. When prospect of war as the aftermath of Napoleon's disastrous Russian campaign was looming in Berlin, he fled to Rudolfstadt, a quiet little town, to work on his dissertation in peace. He submitted his dissertation to the University of Jena and received the degree of the Doctor of Philosophy in 1813. The work was later published as *The Fourfold Root of the Principle of Sufficient Reason*, which Schopenhauer would always prescribe as an essential reading for the proper understanding of his chief work *The World as Will and Representation*. When he told his mother about 'The Fourfold Root' she made a joke that the book seemed to belong to a pharmacy. He responded that it would still be read, when none of her works will be available, indicating that she would only be remembered as his mother and not due to her own works of fiction. Although an arrogant claim, but this prophesy by the proud young philosopher has come true. No one remembers Johanna Schopenhauer, the authoress. Her works of fiction are long lost having suffered the fate of dated literary exertions of minor writers. After the completion of his university studies, Schopenhauer had returned to Weimar to board with his mother for a few months. The old quarrels often broke out between them as he behaved too arrogantly towards a literary friend of hers also lodging there and was overly critical of her reckless spending and life-style.

She expressed her own critical assessment of her son's difficult personality in a letter and suggested to him to move away. Thus Schopenhauer left his mother's house and never to see her again in her remaining 24 years. He never again attempted to live with anyone for the rest of his own 46 years. There were some fringe benefits of this last sojourn with his mother. He was able to have some meetings with Goethe, who was on friendly terms with Johanna, whose genius he greatly admired. He had opportunities to show his works to Goethe, whose compliments boosted his morale. In Weimar this time, Frederick Mayer, the well-known Indologist sparked in Schopenhauer an interest in Hindu and Buddhist thought, which initiated his life-long involvement with Eastern philosophy.

THE INDEPENDENT SCHOLAR BEGINS HIS VOCATION

After parting with his mother, Schopenhauer looked for a conducive place to live and compose the outlines of his philosophical system. His choice fell on Dresden, a city with great natural surroundings, museums, art galleries and theatre as well as home to some writers and scholars. He had received his part of his father's inheritance which promised a comfortable financial situation. Thus the young scholar established his residence in Dresden to enjoy his independence, solitude and reasonable social life and to work on the composition of his *magnum opus*.

After completing an essay on the theory of colours in his partnership with Goethe on this subject, Schopenhauer sat down to write his chief work *The World as Will and Representation* which was completed after four years' labour in 1818. Not much is known of his life in Dresden in these years, the only source of information being his intellectual diary. However, this diary is more about his thoughts and intellectual development than about his personal life. It is easy to surmise that he was having difficulties in having friends and becoming increasingly proud of his intellectual superiority to the common mass of humanity he called philistines. Among his acquaintances he had a few minor literary figures of the area, but his manner was haughty and uncompromising. He was already full of the vanity that he was accused of all his life. But perhaps this pride is necessary for one whose work will long be rejected by the reading public and scholarly peers and who had to carry on his lonely march towards philosophical originality and excellence. Perhaps it is not easy to be a philosopher without having some armour of pride as well as a deep love of one's mission in order to survive the indifference or rejection of the so-called practical-minded folks, the people Schopenhauer often calls philistines. How could one have a great mind without knowing it, he asks in his diary. Schopenhauer was sure of the greatness of his *magnum opus* and would remain confident about its lasting value for centuries to come despite its initial lack of sales and indifferent reception by the university scholars. This work completed at age 30 by the author, was only supplemented and elaborated in his subsequent writings. It was never altered, amended or modified. Schopenhauer would remain sure of its perfection and excellence as a substantive contribution to philosophy requiring no modifications at all.

A SOLITARY PHILOSOPHICAL QUEST

Before his book was even out of the print shop, Schopenhauer travelled to Italy, to have a well-deserved vacation. He was in Venice for a few weeks and from there off to Bologna, Florence and Rome. He would always visit theatre and opera, a life-long habit with him, which he regarded as essential for a creative understanding of life and human nature. He was more inclined to have social contact with the English fellow travellers, for he spoke English like a native. The Germans, some of whom had heard about his conceit, eccentricity and tough demeanour would avoid him for the most part. He did not think highly of Italians or Catholics and their religious devotions. The habit of too much praying was likened by him to begging one's way to heaven rather than earning it through moral deeds alone. In May, 1819 he had to return to Germany to safeguard his investments. He was able to recover all of his invested funds from a bankrupt Danzig firm, whereas his mother had earlier agreed on a settlement, which awarded her only 30 percent of her investment. This incident shows that Schopenhauer was not lacking in the business acumen which his father had bequeathed to him. But since all his energies were devoted to philosophy as a higher calling he had no real interest in a business career.

On his return home, he inquired about a prospective university teaching career from Heidelberg, Göttingen and Berlin. He finally chose the University of Berlin where he qualified to be a privat-dozent (private lecturer), such lecturership being the first step towards a university teaching career in Germany. He was not successful in attracting a significant number of students to his lectures, primarily because he had purposely scheduled his lectures at exactly the same time as those of Hegel. Due to his suspicious and unfriendly nature, he soon was on bad terms with his academic colleagues. On his own part, he developed a dislike for academic hypocrisy, pedantry and politics. An essay in his *Parerga and Paralipomena* entitled 'Philosophy in the Universities' gives us a glimpse of Schopenhauer's bitter experience with academia, and his low opinion of professor-philosophers.

All his life Schopenhauer was very sensitive to noise. As he mentions in his essay on 'Din and Noise' (PP-II, 642–645), noise in his environment had been a daily torment to him. Meanwhile in Berlin, a seamstress pressed charges against him for pushing her down the stairs after he found her in the hallway across from his rooms, chatting with two other women. It was a very unpleasant and costly affair for Schopenhauer, who had to pay her an annual compensation ordered by a court for the rest of her life. It shows that his intolerance of others and quarrelsome nature was getting out of hand during his stay in Berlin. He took another extended trip to Italy in 1821 and returned to Munich, where he lived in isolation for a year or so. He shifted his residence several times from 1819 to 1831 in different German cities finally returning to Berlin. This period was full of isolation and professional disappointments. His book had evoked hardly any response and his proposals to translate first Hume and then Kant were not accepted. In 1931 when cholera broke out in Berlin, true to his cautious nature, Schopenhauer immediately fled to Frankfurt. Unfortunately, the same pestilence in Berlin claimed Hegel. After a brief attempt to live in Mannheim for health reasons, he finally settled down in Frankfurt where he was to remain until his death.

THE SAGE OF FRANKFURT

Schopenhauer seemed to put some of the turmoils and disappointments of his mid-life behind him having found consolation in his own philosophy. To prevent ourselves from being very unhappy we should not desire to be very happy. As he says in *Parerga and Paralipomena*:

> A happy life is impossible; the best that man can attain is a 'heroic life', such as lived by one who struggles against overwhelming odds in someway and some affair that will benefit the whole of

mankind, and who in the end triumphs, although he obtains a poor reward or none at all. (PP-II, 322)

Having resolved to live for philosophy rather than by it, he settled down to obtain the inner rewards of contemplation. After a lull of 17 years he produced a new work called the *Will in Nature* (1836). It was followed by an essay 'On the Freedom of the Will' which received a prize from the Royal Norwegian Academy after a competition. His next entry for a similar competition by the Royal Danish Academy was rejected which evoked a great deal of bitterness in him. The Academy also chided him for using very strong language regarding his fellow philosophers especially his unjustified attacks on Hegel and Fichte which were unbecoming within a scholarly debate. However, he published both these prize and non-prize essays under the title *The Two Fundamental Problems of Ethics* (1841), the preface to which expresses the author's full fury against the Royal Danish Academy. Schopenhauer's excessive pride at the success of his work with the Norwegian Academy and undue bitterness at the rejection of his essay by the Danish Academy tell us not only about his sensitive nature but also about his deep disappointment over the fact that the academic community had failed to take adequate notice of his chief work *The World as Will and Representation* (1818). In 1844 the second and enlarged edition of his chief work was published in two volumes.

Schopenhauer's daily regimen during the last phase of his life has been recorded in all of his biographies. In his own way he applied the wisdom of life that he expounds in his later popular works to his own living. He lived in very simple rented apartments of no more than two rooms. The place was always plainly but elegantly furnished. Of course, he possessed a library of a highly selective collection. Only in his fifties he acquired furniture of his own. Besides portraits of some Western thinkers and writers, especially Kant and Goethe he had a gilded bronze statue of the Buddha on a console. On his desk stood a bust of Kant. He had no craving for innumerable objects or for a typically aristocratic life of luxury. He watched his money but he was neither extravagant nor a miser. By the time he died, he had doubled his father's inheritance by prudent investments. He supported some of his poor relatives and often contributed to charities. Although he was an outspoken critic of human follies, weaknesses and cravings, he was utterly compassionate towards the disadvantaged sections of society. He was one of the rare Western thinkers who spoke out for the importance and the rights of animals. 'Were there no dogs, I wouldn't want to live' is a thought-provoking saying of his. He always had a dog as his companion since his Göttingen days. A dog that he had 1840 onwards was named 'Atman' which in Sanskrit means the soul or the spirit of all beings. 'Atman is the *Brahman* (Being)' is the primary insight of Vedanta philosophy which very much influenced Schopenhauer. 'Atman' was followed by 'Butz' who outlived his master, and was provided for in Schopenhauer's will.

At this stage of his life, Schopenhauer lost all fascination for travelling, which he calls needful for the youth but unnecessary for the old. He had a very disciplined, organized and moderate life-style at the prime of his life. The daily routine resembled that of Kant in many ways, except that Schopenhauer was not an early bird. Schopenhauer attributes Kant's eventual senility in his old age to his habit of rising too early and working too much on intellectual tasks. Schopenhauer emphasizes that more than four hours of intellectual exertion is unnatural and excessive. Accordingly, he woke up between 7 a.m. and 8 a.m., took a sponge bath and had a coffee prepared by himself. He had instructed his housekeeper not to disturb him in the mornings. He devoted the whole morning to writing or difficult intellectual tasks. He never received any guests in the mornings but later, during his years of fame, he admitted some visitors after 11 a.m. At 12 noon, he would play his flute for half an hour, and, meticulously dressed, would arrive at the Englischer Hof to dine. Some biographers have expressed amazement at his large appetite. Besides his own explanation that he possessed a head larger than others, we may surmise that it was due to his habit of missing breakfast. After dinner he returned home, had a coffee and took a nap for an hour or so. Around four in the evening he would set out for a walk, rain or shine. He usually walked through the countryside, not too far from his quarters, Atman always following him. Schopenhauer regarded long walks essential for the health of one's body as well as one's mind. After the conclusion of his walk he would go to a reading room and glance over the day's English and French newspapers. He would always give a careful perusal to *The Times*. There are numerous citations in his later writings from *The Times* regarding crime reports, executions and mundane occurrences from which he draws profound philosophical conclusions. This is one more instance of the closeness of his philosophy to the everyday living of human beings. In the late evenings, he would often go to the theatre or an opera. Later on when he grew deaf he was deprived of this pleasure. After his visit to a theatre, he would have a cold supper at the restaurant again. At his return home, he would do some light reading followed by a reading of a few passages from his anthology of the Upanishads. Then he would sleep for nine hours for he believed that his brain required at least that much rest.

FAME AT LAST

It was only in the last decade of his life that Schopenhauer's works attracted notice and he enjoyed the warmth of recognition. Some readers had begun to admire his writings in the late 1840s. Julius Frauenstadt, a scholar and a writer, met Schopenhauer in 1847 and became his ardent disciple and friend. Frauenstadt worked tirelessly to spread the ideas of his master through his articles in periodicals and newspapers, and kept him informed of the citations and mentions of his philosophy in the press and in academic circles. The political disturbances of 1847 onwards convinced Schopenhauer that democrats represented mob rule and he was definitely against the insurgency and in favour of republican forces of law and order. It is for the welfare of the widows of the soldiers killed in this revolution that he left the bulk of his estate in his will. He worked for over six years on his two volumes of miscellaneous writings later published as *Parerga and Paralipomena* (1851). The failure of the 1848 revolution, the despondency of the public in its aftermath, the decline of Hegelianism, all caused favourable conditions for Schopenhauer's emergence as a popular writer. It was his *Parerga and Paralipomena*, a work designed for popular readership rather than academics that brought him his well-deserved recognition. Among his committed admirers and disciples were Lindner, a lawyer from Munich, Adam von Doss, an editor of a popular liberal newspaper, Dorguth, an elderly councilor of Justice from Magdeburg (who published several tracts in praise of the master), and many others from all walks of life. What brought him academic notice was an article published in *The Westminster Review* in English, entitled 'Iconoclasm in German Philosophy'. The article was translated into German by the wife of the above-mentioned Lindner, the editor of *Vossische Zeitung*. The article recognized Schopenhauer's original contribution to philosophy in its opposition to the dominant transcendentalism in German philosophy and admired

Schopenhauer's powerful writing style. Dr W. Gwinner became another important disciple of the philosopher in 1854. He would later write the first and most authoritative biography of Schopenhauer. In the mid-1850s numerous admirers from different cities were regularly corresponding with Schopenhauer, and he was receiving a large number of visitors. Some would dine at the Englischer Hof, just to catch a glimpse of their admired thinker. After the publication of *Parerga and Paralipomena*, he did not wish to author any more original works, but worked on supplementing and refining his previous writings. The popularity of *Parerga and Paralipomena* was responsible for a heightened interest in Schopenhauer's previous works. A third edition of the *World as Will and Representation* appeared in 1859, second editions of *Will in Nature* in 1854, and *Two Fundamental Problems of Ethics* in 1860. These new editions carried honorariums and book sales were increasing. He actually made some money as a writer. Schopenhauer revelled in his approbation and showed hardly any modesty in his reactions. In 1855, the French painter Lunteschüz did his portrait. In 1856 he was painted by Goebel. Both these portraits were copied in engravings. Lastly, Elizabeth May of Berlin made a bust of him, which has been a very well-crafted sculpture. All these mementos along with the remainder of his library that survived the bombing of World War II are kept in *Schopenhauer Archives* in *Stadt und Universitätsbibliothek* in Frankfurt. Finally, the German universities also paid some attention to him. Leipzig offered a prize for the best essay on his philosophy.

He was healthy and active to the last. His growing deafness was the only sign of age. But one day in April, 1860 he had an attack of palpitations and shortness of breath during his usual rapid-paced walk. This happened again in September; he fell ill with inflammation of lungs but recovered. After a few days he had a fainting spell. Next morning, he woke up normally, took his sponge bath and had his coffee. The housekeeper came in, opened the window and abstained herself as per her usual instructions. A few moments later the physician came and found him dead on the sofa. Obviously the death was quick and painless. As he descended into that dark valley where all roads meet, his own words seemed to come true: 'Dying is the moment of that liberation from the one-sidedness of . . . an individuality which does not constitute the innermost kernel of our being . . . As a rule the death of every good person is peaceful and gentle' (W-II, 508).

CHAPTER TWO

THE WORLD AS REPRESENTATION

Schopenhauer begins his chief work *WWR* with a profound statement 'This world is my representation'. This assertion acknowledges that the stuff that the world is made up of is not all existing and material things put together, but it is composed of representations of each and every knowing and living being, although only human beings receive these representations reflectively. Schopenhauer says that man's recognition of the world as representation is the beginning of philosophical thought for an individual. Representation is the translation of the German term *vorstellung* the literal meaning of which is 'what stands before'. Representations are the meaningful images of the worldly phenomena that stand before the mind's eye. The world is nothing but a representation of a representing being, that is, man. This connection between the representation and the representing being, that is between the object and the subject, is a form more general than any other form including those that are modes of the principle of sufficient reason such as time, space and causality.

> Therefore no other truth is more certain, more independent of all the others, and less in need to proof than this, namely that everything that exists for knowledge, and hence the whole of this world, is only object in relation to the subject, perception of the perceiver, in a word, representation. (W-I, 3)

Thus the subject–object dichotomy or subject–object bifurcation of reality that Heidegger attempts to bypass in his way of thinking is the most obvious and fundamental truth for Schopenhauer. This truth is not new, Schopenhauer points out. It was embedded in Cartesian mode of subject-ism and more clearly stated by Berkeley who argued that to exist and to perceive or be perceived is one and the same thing. This truth was also present in the ancient Vedanta philosophy of India which maintained that 'existence and perceptibility are convertible terms' (W-I, 4).

To consider the world as representation is obviously a one-sided view, Schopenhauer warns. The world will also be recognized as 'will' after an initial but thorough consideration of it as representation. Representation as an essential aspect of the world strikes us first as we begin to treat the world as a philosophical problem but only a deeper reflection reveals that the world is a phenomenon of one's will. But the first thing should come first, and Schopenhauer resolves to focus on that aspect of the world which is representation in Book I of *WWR*.

The subject is that which knows all things but cannot be known. It is the essential condition of all appearance, for there can be no object without the existence of a subject. In so far as one knows anything, one finds oneself as a subject. But the body is the immediate object for all human beings. The body being an object among the objects is subject to forms of knowledge such as time, space and causality. However, the subject that knows is not subordinate to these forms of space, time and causality. Thus subject and object are two essential, necessary and inseparable halves of the world as representation.

According to Schopenhauer, the separation of these halves is inconceivable even in thought and they limit each other. Where the object begins the subject ends is problematic and vice versa. The universal forms of any object, that is, space, time and causality reside a priori in our consciousness as Kant explained. Schopenhauer adds to the Kantian insight that the principle of sufficient reason is the common expression or umbrella term for all these forms of the object. Thus every object is subordinate to the principle of sufficient reason (see the section on 'the Principle of Sufficient Reason' below). It is a principle which explains that every object 'stands in a necessary relation' to other objects. That is, no object is a stand-alone object; each object is determined as well as determining with respect to other objects. Schopenhauer comes close here to the Buddhist theory of co-dependent co-origination (*pratitya samutpada*) of all entities.

INTUITIVE REPRESENTATION

According to Schopenhauer, abstract representations are constituted of concepts. The capacity for these has often been called reason (*Vernunft*).

What distinguishes man from the animal is the capacity of having abstract representations. It is however the intuitive representation that covers the possibility of all experience and the entire visible world. Schopenhauer acknowledges the contribution of Kant in so far as he showed that the conditions or forms of the visible world, namely, time and space, can be separated from their content in thought, and also be perceived. This intuition of time and space does not come about as a result of experience; rather all experience is dependent on it. They are known in an a-priori intuition and serve as laws of experience. Schopenhauer adds on to this insight of Kant regarding time and space as the universal forms of intuition by maintaining that the principle of sufficient reason, which determines experience in terms of causality and motivation, appears in the forms of space and time in a special form, named by Schopenhauer as 'ground of being'.

Among the various forms part and parcel of the principle of sufficient reason, that of time is the simplest, and it is time that denotes the essence of this principle 'succession is the whole essence and nature of time' (W-I, 8). Thus Schopenhauer accepts Aristotle's doctrine of time, unlike Heidegger who emphasizes the existential ground of time. However, Schopenhauer does regard time and space as intuitive forms of human representation. In the principle of sufficient reason, the form of matter or the law of causality governs the contents of the forms of time and space. Schopenhauer explains that matter really means causality because 'its being is its acting'. Something that acts does so in terms of time and space. The action of the matter upon its immediate object, which is also matter, conditions the perception. And thus matter exists only in the perception. Matter is nothing but cause and effect; 'its being is its acting.' Schopenhauer mentions that, in German, substance of a material thing is called *wirklichkeit* (literally, effectiveness), which is a much better term than *Realität* (reality). He remarks in a footnote with the help of a quote from Seneca, that ordinary expressions of a language sometimes contain a deep philosophical insight into the nature of things. This is why Heidegger often resorts to etymological analysis to obtain clues for philosophizing about the Being of things. This is one reason that Heidegger calls language 'the house of Being'. Thus the essential connection between matter, whose being is its acting, and the forms of time and space is explained by Schopenhauer as follows: 'Time and space . . . each by itself, can be represented in intuition even without matter; but matter cannot be so represented without time and space' (W-I, 9).

Since the representation of the object exists only for the subject, the same way each special class of representations exist for a commensurately special disposition within the subject. The subjective correlative of time and space was named 'pure sensibility' by Kant, which Schopenhauer accepts with a proviso that sensibility may not be the most appropriate term here for it seems to presuppose matter. As pointed out above, the subject can have the intuition of time and space irrespective of matter. The subjective correlative of matter or causality is named as 'understanding' by Schopenhauer. Understanding is primarily the understanding of causality. 'All causality, hence all matter, and consequently the whole of reality is only for the understanding . . . the ever present manifestation of understanding is perception' (W-I, 11). What Schopenhauer emphasizes is that perception is not merely a by-product of the senses but of the intellect. The understanding of cause and effect is a prerequisite upon which depend all perception and thus all experience. The knowledge of the causal law is never the result of experience. Knowledge of causality is independent of all experience and has an a-priori character as experience depends on it. This knowledge is already there in all perception.

That perception is based on a knowledge of causality should not be taken as a reason for assuming a causal relationship between the object and the subject. Schopenhauer warns that such erroneous assumptions can give rise to foolish controversies that question the reality of the external world, as well as those between dogmatic realism and idealism. As explained above, causality precedes perception and experience as their pre-condition. Causality is not a by-product of experience. The subject and object precede all knowledge and the principle of sufficient reason applies only to the object and not to the subject. This principle applies solely to the form of the object or to the 'universal mode of all objective existence'. But the subject which is the necessary correlative of the object, and pre-supposed by the object, remains outside the bounds of the principle of sufficient reason. Schopenhauer responds to the possible controversies on this issue as follows:

The whole world of objects is and remains representation and is for this reason wholly and forever conditioned by the subject; in other words, it has transcendental ideality. But it is not on that account falsehood or illusion; it presents itself as a series of representations, whose common bond is the principle of sufficient reason. (W-I, 15)

For the human subject, the body is its immediate object. The body is a representation that is the starting-point in the perception of the world or for the subject's knowledge. The subjective correlative of the causality is the understanding, which is affected by the sensations and changes in the body, which is why Schopenhauer calls the body the 'immediate object'. But the body is not an ordinary object or object in the fullest sense. Schopenhauer explains that there are two conditions for the possibility of perception. First, it happens due to the proper function of understanding to make sense of the visible world based on the law of causality. Secondly, it happens because of the sensibility of the animal bodies, that is, due to special nature of some certain bodies to function as immediate object of the subject. Thus the body does not itself appear as object in the fullest sense, but other bodies affecting it or acting on it become direct objects through it. But this endowment of understanding is not confined to man alone. 'All animals, even the most imperfect, have understanding, for they all know objects, and this knowledge as motive determines their movements' (W-I, 21). What is special about man is that he has 'abstract concepts of reason' in addition to the understanding. The concepts of reason work on what is supplied by the understanding; they can never bring about understanding which intuitively comprehends the forces and laws of nature. Thus Schopenhauer warns that it is not proper to downplay the understanding in animals by subsuming it under the name of instinct. The instinct is something other than understanding and than the faculty of reason.

ABSTRACT REFLECTION OR CONCEPTS OF REASON

In addition to the immediate representation of perception, man has reflection or ability to have concepts of reason, whose content is based on perceptual knowledge and is related to this perception. In other words, reflection or conceptual activity of reason is always a development or further sophistication of the perceptual knowledge; it is never detached from or something entirely other than the immediate representation that one has of the worldly reality. Interestingly, Heidegger uses a similar distinction between 'understanding' and 'interpretation' as part of Dasein's disclosedness or reality. In pure perception everything is clear and virgin, also certain and indisputable. But in abstract reflection of the faculty of reason, doubt and error appear invariably. Schopenhauer remarks that 'in the representation of the abstract, error can reign for thousands of years, impose its iron yoke on whole nations, stifle the noblest impulses of mankind' (W-I, 35). The perennial concepts and hardened interpretations hold their sway for centuries over different cultures. After all, all these concepts were invented by someone's faculty of reason and subsequently found general acceptance within a specific tradition. Heidegger says in the introduction to his *Being and Time* that it is the business of philosophy to re-examine the perennial concepts of a tradition and to let these concepts display their birth certificates and calls this inquiry the 'positive destruction of the history of ontology'. Schopenhauer here is alluding to the same powerful historical spell on a whole tradition. He says that 'reflection' is an appropriate term for conceptual knowledge that is derived from the knowledge of perception and is truly a particular reflection of the perception, which nevertheless has a role to play in the development of man's reality. Schopenhauer points out that, due to the possession of this rational faculty, man far surpasses animals in wielding his power over nature and the world. But the same rational endowment makes man endure much more suffering than his 'irrational brothers'.

Every step of the way in his philosophy, Schopenhauer compares and contrasts man with the animal to gain insights about human nature. Besides suffering infinitely more than the animal due primarily to his rational faculty, man seldom lives in the present like the animal does nor is led merely by the motives at hand. 'He carries out considered plans, or acts in accordance with maxims, without regard to his surroundings or to the accidental impressions of the moment. The animal feels and perceives; man in addition "thinks" and "knows"; both "will"' (W-I, 37). What distinguishes man from the animal is his power of speech which is 'a necessary instrument of his faculty of reason'. Therefore in Greek and in Italian, speech and reason have the same word (*logos, discourso*). The German word for reason *Vernunft* is rooted in *vernehmen* which means 'being aware of ideas'.

The concepts are based on representations of perception, but differ from them in many ways. Therefore we cannot have a perceptive or clear-cut knowledge of the nature of concepts, nor can they be validated in experience. 'They can only be conceived not perceived, and only the effects that man produces through them are objects of experience proper. Such effects are language, deliberate and planned action and science, and what results from all these' (W-I, 39). As pointed out above, concepts are rooted in a necessary relation to the representations of perception. Therefore, they are, in fact, 'the representations of representation'. Thus concepts are never free of the principle of sufficient reason, which applies to them in a special form. The whole nature of concepts or abstract reflections abides in the relations expressed in them by the law of sufficient reason. One abstract representation may have its relation to another representation which may be its ground. This in turn, may again be an intuitive representation or a concept. However, the series of grounds of knowledge ultimately must end or find their ground in knowledge of perception.

Schopenhauer points out that every concept due to its character as an abstract representation has a range or sphere that it covers, even when it is an abstract representation pertaining to a single real object. Thus the sphere of a concept has something in common with other concepts, or may overlap them. Each concept at the same time has what others do not. Imitating the style of Euler, Schopenhauer demonstrates the overlapping and distinctiveness of related concepts in figures. For example, the sphere of 'animal' contains the sphere of 'horse', of 'angle' contains 'right angle', obtuse angle' and 'acute angle' which are themselves exclusive concepts. Schopenhauer explains that when we recognize the relations among concepts, a judgement takes place. 'All combinations of concepts may be referred to these cases, and from them can be derived a whole theory of judgements . . . From them may also be derived the properties of judgements' (W-I, 44). Kant based his categories of understanding on such properties of judgements.

Reason works only on what it has received from the representations of perception. In itself, it has nothing but empty forms. Schopenhauer boils down the logical laws of pure rational knowledge to just four principles 'the principle of identity, of contradiction, of excluded middle, and of sufficient reason of knowledge'. The rest of the logic is not 'perfectly pure rational knowledge' since it presupposes and builds on the already established relations and combinations of the spheres of concepts (W-I, 50). To know means to have within the power of the mind, judgements which have their ground of knowledge in something in the world, the judgements which are true due to their correspondence to the actual representations of perception. According to Schopenhauer, the abstract knowledge may be called rational knowledge (*Wissen*). This knowledge is conditioned by the faculty of reason which only man possesses.

THE PRINCIPLE OF SUFFICIENT REASON

How can we account for a principle that would explain the ground of things adequately? There must be a principle that elucidates the necessary relation of every entity or event to every other. Although the roots of the quest for a principle of ground can be traced as far back as Plato and Aristotle, it was pursued in the thought of several major thinkers throughout the history of Western philosophy. In eighteenth century it was widely discussed and Leibniz called it a 'first principle'. In our age, Heidegger discusses this issue in his own way, by referring to Being as ground in *Essence of Reasons* (*Vom Wesen des Grundes*, 1929). Schopenhauer found this principle crucial for the understanding of his theory of representation. His interest in the principle of ground began with his doctoral thesis *On the Fourfold Roots of the Principle of Sufficient Reason* (*FRPSR*), which he published in 1813, five years before the publication of *WWR*. In his chief work he repeatedly mentions that *FRPSR* must be thoroughly read by all serious readers before beginning a study of *WWR*. He keeps referring to his first publication as the 'Introductory Essay' throughout the first book of *WWR*. He found *FRPSR* so important for his system on the whole, that he published its second expanded edition in 1847.

The principle of sufficient reason, which penetrates several methods of knowledge and a-priori principles, can simply be stated as 'Nothing is without a reason for its being.' This is the version of the principle given by Christian Wolff that Schopenhauer considers as the most comprehensive. He quotes Aristotle's observation that 'all knowledge which is intellectual . . . deals with causes and principles' (*Metaph*, V, 1) to conclude that 'all things must have their reason' (*FRPSR*, 5). The principle also means that nothing is self-caused or autonomous. All things appear from a network of causation. Everything relates to other things and all things due to the fact that each entity has as its reason of being, another entity which is its cause and explains it. The other entity has yet another as its cause and explanation and so on. And this chain of causes goes on forever, ruling out any self-caused being. However, the cause is only one of the four ways in which a thing relates to its ground. According to Schopenhauer, besides the causal necessity, there could be a logical or a mathematical or a moral necessity of the being of a thing or event. The four roots or the four forms of the principle were never comprehensively identified in the history of the quest for grounds of being of things in the history of Western philosophy according to Schopenhauer. Aristotle's fourfold division of the causes merely dealt with only one of the aspects of the principle, namely the causal aspect. The blind adherence of the scholastic philosophers to Aristotle's emphasis on cause as the only necessary aspect of reason resulted in a confusion about the principle. The confusions largely pertain to the distinction between the causal and the logical grounds of things. The same confusion appears in Descartes whose proof of the existence of God displays a muddling between cause and the ground of knowledge, between the empirical and the epistemological (*FRPSR*, 6–13). According to Schopenhauer, Hegel's entire philosophy is a 'monstrous amplification of the ontological proof' (*FRPSR*, 13). Kant's distinction between the formal (logical) and the material (transcendental), which meant that every proposition must have its ground and every thing must have its ground, was an important step away from confusion, but it still did not capture the full range of the forms of this principle under one umbrella. In sum, Schopenhauer maintains that none of his predecessors have given a complete and comprehensive account of the principle and its application. Some have even wasted their energies in seeking a proof or the ground of the principle itself.

(1) *The Causal Form*: Schopenhauer maintains that the two distinct applications of the principle of sufficient reason acknowledged by Kant and his followers are by no means an exhaustive account of the principle. Their recognition that judgements or propositions must have a ground, and the changes undergone by objects must have a cause, do not capture the fuller range of this principle's application. The reason that three equal sides of a triangle must produce three equal angles is neither logical nor causal necessity (*FRPSR*, 29). The reason in this case is instinctively recognized and is mathematical. Schopenhauer points out that all representations are objects of the subject. But representations have an orderly connection, whose form is determinable a priori. Thus nothing is self-standing, or independent of other things among the objects.

The principle of sufficient reason explains this connection in its formal generality. These inter-connections or inter-relations fall into four classes or four forms of necessity: namely causal, logical, mathematical and moral. The first class of objects and the form of the principle applicable to it have to do with the representations of perception which constitute our experience. This class includes the most obvious objects that occupy space and time. The representations of perception emerge due to their impact on the sensations in the body of the subject, and are perceived through the forms of space and time. Space and time, together create persistence and succession which constitute reality. If there were no space, there will be no persistence of objects, and if there were no time, there will be no succession or change. Time and space themselves are not perceivable; the subject perceives what fills time and space, that is, matter. Matter itself is endless, but the dimensions of time and space help us conceive distinct material objects and changes in them. This combination of space and time is the primary function of understanding. In this kind of objects, the principle of sufficient reason operates as the law of causality. It is this law that connects together through the process of becoming, all objects of perception. The changing state of an object or new objects appear through a causal sequence, the preceding state being the cause, and the following being the effect. However, 'it is quite wrong to call the objects themselves as the causes, instead of the states . . . because objects not only contain form and quality, but matter also, which has neither beginning nor end' (*FRPSR*, 40). Schopenhauer explains that the chain of causes and effects does not impact on matter within which all changes occur.

Understanding creates perceptions of space and time or the objective world without the participation of reflection or abstract reasoning. The sole and proper function of understanding is to apprehend causal relations. Schopenhauer maintains that this basic function of understanding exists in all animals as well as human beings. Thus Kant's attribution of 12 complicated categories to understanding is wrong. The law of causality has a twofold function, according to Schopenhauer. It organizes the relation or inter-connection among the material objects. At the same time, it enables the subject to bring material things into being through a process of the understanding. Understanding merely apprehends reality through an immediate causal apprehension. Schopenhauer points out that between the volition of the mind and action of the body there is no causal relation. Volition (will) and action are the same thing within the human subject. It is our point of view that treats them differently. This insight will be the foundation for Schopenhauer's all important concept of 'will' in his later works.

(2) *The Logical Form*: As Schopenhauer will explain at length in *WWR*, man differs from the animal in possessing something over and above mere understanding of causal relations. Man is endowed with reason, that is abstract representations or concepts. The animal does not possess abstract representations which are different from those of perception, and therefore lacks speech. Actions of humans are necessarily governed by cause and effect and so are the actions of animals. However, in case of man, choice is based on a conflict of motives and is produced by his conceptual reasoning. Unlike the animal, his operation of thought, with the assistance of the faculty of speech, produce general conceptions. However, thought is not just the outcome of the presence of abstract representations, but it is based on a combination and separation of such representations, subject to logical constraints and judgements.

For such rational judgements of conceptual relations, the principle of sufficient reason assumes a new form, which Schopenhauer calls the principle of sufficient reason of knowing or the ground of knowing (*FRPSR*, 124). This form of the principle demands that if a judgement is to be knowledge, it must have a ground. It is this ground or reason that makes this judgement true or false. The judgements of inter-connection between concepts may have one of the four grounds: (1) another judgement may be its ground, which gives it formal or 'logical truth'; Schopenhauer says that the 'intrinsic truth' typically invoked by the proofs of God's existence would be an absurdity; (2) a conceptual judgement may have its ground in perceptual representations, which accords it a 'material truth'; (3) a judgement might be based on 'the conditions of all possible experience', making it have a 'transcendental truth'. An example of transcendental truth is 'nothing happens without a cause' or '3×7=21'. (4) Finally, a judgement may be rooted on the formal conditions of all thinking based in reason, which may give it 'metalogical truth'. There are only four such metalogical judgements, namely (i) a subject is equal to the sum of its predicates; (ii) a predicate can't be both affirmed or denied to a subject; (iii) one of the two contradictory predicates must apply to every subject; and (iv) truth is the reference of a judgement to something outside of it (*FRPSR*, 128).

(3) *Mathematical Form*: The third class of objects are space and time themselves which are objects of pure intuition for the subject. Following Kant, Schopenhauer maintains that human subjects are able to comprehend space and time as pure non-empirical intuitions. This class of representation differs from ordinary perception in which space and time show the presence of matter and causality becomes objective. In this intuition, the relationship between space and time, the fact that one conditions the other, is intelligible to the subject in a peculiar way, which has nothing to do with understanding or reason. The space–time connection is grasped through an a-priori perception. The mode of the principle of sufficient reason operative here is the 'sufficient reason of being'. Schopenhauer subscribes to the notion that in space, each position has a reference to another, one being the ground of the other. In time, every moment is a succession of the preceding moment and time has a single dimension of sequential movement. Here Schopenhauer adopts the traditional Aristotelian notion of 'time as a series of nows'. Heidegger would challenge this notion to assert that both space and time are existential, rather than autonomous. Here Schopenhauer distinguishes this ground of being that produces 'insight' from the ground of knowledge (reason) that produces merely 'conviction'. Geometry and arithmetic depend on this kind of intuition regarding the divisions of space and time. In dealing with axioms in geometry we appeal to the intuition of space, whereas in theorems, a reason of knowing is invoked. But reason of knowing does not explain why if two angles of a triangle are equal, the two opposite sides shall also be equal. Only due to the conviction based on the reason of being, it is known to us intuitively. But this necessity that does not need demonstration, we fully understand the relation between the angles and the sides of a triangle (*FRPSR*, 161). Here it is not a matter of grasping causality or logical justification, but the ground of being of space.

(4) *The Moral Form*: The fourth class of objects is in fact a single object of the subject's own volition, which is behind all deliberate activity of the subject. It becomes an object of knowledge in a peculiar inner way within time alone, and not in space. Human subject is

aware of himself or herself as a subject that wills. One is aware of one's volition, one's decisions, and one comprehends why one made a certain decision in wanting or doing something. One can identify one's motives as the ground of acting one way or the other. However, the subject cannot itself become the object of knowledge. It knows itself not as knowing but as a willing being. What introspection shows us is never knowing but our willing. Schopenhauer maintains that it is impossible to detach the subject that knows from the subject that wills; both are part of the sense of 'I' that man has. The motive is unlike other causes which operate in the external world. The effect produced by the motive can be explained indirectly just as we know other causes from the outside, but at the same time is known quite directly from inside (*FRPSR*, 171). Thus motivation can be called causality viewed from within. In this sphere of human volition, the principle of sufficient reason assumes the form of 'principle of the sufficient reason of acting' or as the law of motivation. It indicates that willed acts can be explained in terms of motives.

CHAPTER THREE

THE WORLD AS WILL

In the first book of the *WWR*, Schopenhauer considers the general form of representation as well as the part played by concepts in the representation of perception. In the second book the question is posed regarding the real significance of the representations of perception. Why is it that representations do not just slide past us as meaningless images but engage us and absorb us completely in their world? Why is it that their interplay is not a mere picture show but the very ground of our quest for meaning in the world? Schopenhauer suggests that philosophy cannot be satisfied with a mere logical arrangement of representations but it seeks to comprehend the significance and nature of the thing-in-itself, as much as it can be known by a human mind. 'We are not satisfied with knowing that we have representations, that they are such and such, that they are connected according to this or that law . . . We want to know the significance of these representations' (W-I, 98).

WILL AND THE BODY

However, what the world is in addition to being a network of representations would never emerge as an issue if the inquirer himself were no more than a knowing subject or what Schopenhauer calls 'winged cherub without a body'. But man finds himself rooted in a world, considers himself an individual and has a body. The world as representations appears to him in and through his body, which is the starting point of all perceptions. The body is obviously also a representation and an object among objects. Its actions and movements are observable just as the changes undergone by other objects of perception. But the meaning of the actions and movements of his own body are available to the individual in a manner quite different from his perceptions and dealings with other objects of the world. The body's experiences are known directly and internally. The usual difference between intention and the act does not apply within the body. The changes of the other objects are understood to an extent on the basis of causes, stimuli, motives and laws of nature whereas actions and manifestations of the body are understood in a more direct and comprehensive manner by the individual.

What gives the human subject of knowledge the key to his self-understanding is named 'will' by Schopenhauer. 'This and this alone gives him the key to his own phenomenon, reveals to him the significance and shows him the inner mechanism of his being, his actions, his movements' (W-I, 100). The human being exists as an individual through his identity with the body. This body is endowed to him in two different ways; first, as a representation or as an object among objects, and second as something which is known immediately and directly, that is, as the will. Every act of the individual's will is at the same time a movement of his body. The act of will and the action of the body do not have a causal relation. But they are one and the same thing. The action of the body can be called an act of will objectified and available to perception. Indeed, the whole body is objectified will, or will that has become representation. Willing and acting are distinct only in reflection; in fact, they are one. The so-called resolutions of the will (e.g. New Year's resolutions) are not real acts of the will but mere deliberations of reason or mere intentions. They are acts of will only when they are actually carried out. Schopenhauer mentions that the identity between the body and the will is visible in the fact that every strong movement of the will or strong emotion agitates the body. It affects the inner works and parts of the body directly and can even make it dysfunctional at times.

This does not mean that one knows one's will as a whole or as a unity or completely in its nature. The knowledge of the will is an immediate knowledge which cannot be detached from the knowledge one has of one's body. We know our will in individual acts, over time, since time is the form in which the body appears. Thus 'body is the condition of the knowledge of my will.' In other words, the knowledge of the will comes to the individual in a piecemeal fashion through the acts of the body, over the passage of time within one's life-span. Thus self-knowledge is rightly said to be an ongoing process. This message is contained in Socrates' dictum 'know thyself,' which appears in Schopenhauer's terms as 'know thy will.'

Comparable to Schopenhauer's distinction between representational knowledge and bodily knowledge is Heidegger's reference to existential (*existenzial*) and 'existentiell' (*existenziell*) understanding. 'Existentiell' understanding is the one that human being has in and through existing, is a kind of inner knowledge which is different from the understanding of the structural features of existence in general of everything. It seems that Schopenhauer's emphasis on knowledge of the will in one's own person or the knowledge of the will in one's own body as being the backbone of knowledge as such of entities in the world is an insight that has influenced subsequent existential philosophy in general and the contemporary appreciation of the role of self-understanding within human understanding in general. This existentialist approach is different from the one that dismisses all personal insight as subjective bias in the name of acquiring an objective knowledge. Schopenhauer's approach accords due importance to the body and downplays the traditional focus on the mind and its representations as the sole grounds of human knowledge.

Whereas the things and affairs of the world appear in the consciousness as representations, the body appears quite differently, that is, as will. We have a double knowledge from the body, first about its actions and movements due to motives and second, about its suffering due to external impressions. The immediate information about the nature, action and suffering of the body is very different and much more comprehensive than information we have about any other object. Schopenhauer maintains that it is this special relation to a body makes the knowing subject into an 'individual'. The individual is conscious of his body not merely as a representation among all representations but also in a different way, as a will.

Are the things of the world to be taken as mere representations or mere phantoms or can be assigned the same thinghood or will that we are conscious of in ourselves? 'Our knowledge, bound always to individuality . . . necessarily means that everyone can "be" only one thing whereas he can "know" everything else, and it is this very limitation that creates the need for philosophy' (W-I, 104). Being dissatisfied with the simplistic notion of theoretical egoism which must regard all phenomena outside of one's own will as phantoms, human being, encounter the amazing reality of the thinghood of all things through philosophy. Aristotle's insight that philosophy indeed 'begins from wonder' applies here. It is the limitation of certain knowledge to the being of oneself alone, that creates the need for philosophy through which we seek to resolve the enigma of the thinghood of all things or that of the thing-in-itself which may be present in all things in the same way as we know it to be present in us. Schopenhauer charts the course of philosophy to resolve the enigma of thinghood in the following manner.

> The double knowledge which we have of the nature and action of our own body, and which is given in two completely different ways . . . we shall use . . . as a key to the inner being of every phenomenon in nature. We shall judge all objects which are not our own body, and therefore given to our consciousness . . . only as representations. . . . If we set aside their existence as the subject's representation, what still remains over must be, according to its inner nature, the same as what in ourselves we call 'will'. (W-I, 105)

Schopenhauer maintains that no other kind of reality is attributable to the material world. The only reality other than the representations that we find in our consciousness is the will and nothing else.

WILL AS THE BEING OF THINGS

Will is a name given by Schopenhauer to the Being of all existents, but especially the being-in-itself of the body. But it also has to do with willing of this or that action or taking this or that standpoint by the individual. The will shows itself in the voluntary or deliberate movements of the body. These movements are the individual acts of will that have become visible. The acts of the will and the movements of the body occur simultaneously. They are the same, except that the acts of the will are invisible and the movements of the body visible. Schopenhauer cautions that the true and ultimate ground of the acts of the will is not their motives. Motives only determine particular acts of will of a particular time, place and circumstances. Motives do not determine 'that' I will or 'what' I will in general; they do not proclaim the maxim of the whole of one's willing. In other words, 'the whole inner nature of my willing cannot be explained from the motives, but they determine merely its manifestation at a given point of time. This will itself . . . lies outside the province of the law of motivation' (W-I, 106). The establishment of one phenomenon by another, or a deed by a motive, is a different issue from that of the essence-in-itself or ultimate ground of the deed which is the will. The will's appearance cannot take place through something which is not its own by-product.

The will's appearance happens through the body. Therefore the body itself must be a phenomenon of the will and must be related to an individual's will as a whole. Schopenhauer, borrowing Kantian terms, calls the individual's will the individual's 'intelligible character' and its appearance in time as his 'empirical character'. Thus my body is my will's visible form. It is nothing but my will itself. While individual actions of the body come about through the motives, the action in general is an appearance of the will which is itself groundless. Schopenhauer seems to be tracing the steps of the appearance of a particular action beyond the motives and empirical character to the individual's intelligible character or the individual will, which itself is a phenomenon of the will in general, that is groundless. The ground of the last step cannot be spelled out. We ultimately arrive at a level which can be named but cannot be explained. 'The inner nature of everything that appears in this way remains forever unfathomable, and is presupposed by every etiological explanation; it is merely expressed by the name force or law of nature, or when we speak of actions, the name character or will' (W-I, 108). Schopenhauer's name for the ultimate ground or Being is will, which is well chosen by keeping in mind its clearest manifestations as willing and acting within a human individual.

All human beings possess a knowledge of the inner nature of their own phenomenon which is often identified as a feeling. This knowledge of one's own inner being that comes to one as representation through one's actions and through one's body is named as 'will' by Schopenhauer. This will appears as the most immediate knowledge in an individual's consciousness which has not yet acquired the form of representation in which subject and object have assumed distinct character. This will does not become known to the individual in its wholeness but only in its sporadic particular acts. Schopenhauer suggests that a deeper reflection leads us to recognize the will as the key to the knowledge of 'the innermost being of the whole of nature'. In order to resolve the enigma of the being of all existents, we need to transfer the comprehensive knowledge, direct and indirect, that we have of ourselves to all of the phenomena that unfolds for us as representation. We then gain the insight that the will abides not only in men and animals but in all existing things and the so-called forces of nature.

> It is only this application of reflection which no longer lets us stop at the phenomenon, but leads us on to the thing-in-itself . . . But only the will is thing-in-itself; as such it is not 'representation' at all but *toto genere* different therefrom. It is that of which all representation, all object, is the phenomenon . . . It is the innermost essence, the kernel, of every particular thing and also of the whole. It appears in every blindly acting force of nature, and also in the deliberate conduct of man. (W-I, 110)

Schopenhauer explains his chosen name for the being of all beings. Why call it 'will' rather than anything else? Since this thing-in-itself is never an object but all objects are its phenomena, then perhaps we need to borrow its name from an object. But should we do so randomly, and assign it any name whatsoever, or should we look for a phenomenon which best manifests it. This must be 'the most complete' of all the phenomena of this thing-in-itself. What is 'the most distinct, the most developed, the most directly enlightened' of all its phenomena? 'This is precisely man's will' says Schopenhauer. Thus, the name 'will' is the most appropriate one for the thing-in-itself of which all objects are the phenomena.

WILL AND REASON

Schopenhauer claims that 'hitherto the identity of the inner essence of any striving and operating force in nature with (man's) will has not been recognized' (W-I, 111). This is what he has essentially done by naming 'the genus after its most important species'. Furthermore, what is generally called the will has hitherto been understood as something guided by knowledge or faculty of reason. This is a limited view of the will as something subordinate to reason, and an erroneous one according to Schopenhauer. Since the age of the Greeks, the soul has always been identified as primarily the seat of reason and the will as something inferior, subordinate and controlled by reason. Schopenhauer extends the range of the human willing by identifying it with something known to us directly and immediately albeit fuzzily in the consciousness. This is the manifestation of the thing-in-itself within us which is the ground of all our willing and perceiving of representation. It is far superior to knowledge because knowledge serves the ends of the will as a matter of course. However, in case of human entity alone, knowledge can possibly and in rare cases override the machinations of the will within. This is called denial of the will. However, for the most part, it is not knowledge but the will that remains paramount.

The innermost essence of the will in general which is known to us directly is to be transferred to the weaker phenomenon of one's willing. This will accord the required extension to the concept of the will. Schopenhauer says that those who say that just any name will suffice for the thing-in-itself misunderstand his philosophy. If just any random word is used for this Being of things, it would mean that we are referring to a concept which is merely 'inferred' or abstracted or indirectly understood. 'But the word will is . . . by no means an unknown quantity, something reached by inferences and syllogisms, but something known absolutely and immediately' (W-I, 111). Schopenhauer emphasizes that the will as the thing-in-itself is not an abstraction but the will–man relation is fundamental and essential; a glow of the will is ever present in human consciousness; it is known more directly and more immediately than any other knowledge. Heidegger expresses the man–Being relation in a similar fashion. He says that Dasein (Heidegger's term for the human entity) is a being in whose being, being is an ever present issue. For Dasein, Being of beings is not an abstraction, but for Dasein its Being is 'in each case mine'. That means mine-ness and Being as such are intertwined. Schopenhauer says that the concept of will, among all other concepts, is the one that 'has its origin not in the phenomenon, not in the mere representation of perception, but which comes from within, and proceeds from the immediate consciousness of everyone' (W-I, 112). If we refer to a concept of force, we are referring to something unknown or unknowable. But when we say will, we mention something infinitely better known within us.

THE WILL AND THE FORCES OF NATURE

Schopenhauer often refers to the simple categories of the entities of the world, that is, inorganic and organic nature, and within the organic nature, plant life, animals and human life. He calls the grades of will's objectification and links them with Plato's Ideas. A comprehensive discussion of the grades of will's objectification is offered as part of Schopenhauer's philosophy of art and art forms (see Chapter Five). But while referring to the will's objectifications in Book II of *WWR*, he cautions that he has used the term Idea in Platonic sense only, and not in the sense of abstract productions of reason as done so 'wrongly and illegitimately' by Kant (W-I, 129).

At the lowest grade of will's manifestation, that is, in the domain of inorganic matter, a number of universal forces of nature are identifiable. All matter is subject to forces of gravity or impenetrability. These forces govern different categories of matter as 'rigidity, fluidity, elasticity, electricity, magnetism, chemical properties and qualities of every kind' (W-I, 130). Schopenhauer maintains that these natural forces are immediate phenomena of the will, the same way as the conduct of man is. Just as the ultimate man's character is ultimately groundless, so are these forces. That is, these forces are groundless means that they cannot be called the effect or the cause. They are original forces not subject to cause and effect themselves; only their manifestations or particular phenomena have causes. It is therefore wrong to inquire about a cause of gravity or electricity, which are themselves original manifestations of the will and therefore groundless. The natural forces are independent of the chain of causes and effects, which is based on time. Such forces are also timeless. They bequeath the cause with efficacy, or provide it with an ultimate ground, no matter how many times it happens.

Schopenhauer points out that entities at the higher level of will's objectivity are endowed with individuality. In the case of human beings individuality and individual character define a person along with their outward forms of a distinct personality and an individual physique. No animal shows individuality of the type that man does, although in some higher species a trace of it is found. The further we descend to lower grades of the will's objectivity in plant life and in inorganic nature, the individual character disappears into the general character of the species. This is also visible in the sexual and procreative nature of human versus animal gradations of the will. Whereas animals care very little for sexual selection, in man an instinctive sexual selection takes the form of a powerful passion and often becomes an all important consideration. Schopenhauer discusses the passion of love in more detail in his supplementary Volume II of the *WWR* and other later writings (see Chapter Six). His thesis is that all human love between the sexes, the fulfilment of the will's goal of procreation, overwhelms two individuals to a fixation at an instinctive level. At the level of inorganic nature, the individuality of different phenomena is not really visible, but all things express the Idea of their species.

All the phenomena of inorganic nature are manifestations of universally applicable natural forces. Time, space, plurality, determination by cause, do not apply either to the will or to the Ideas or the grades of will's objectification. They belong only to the phenomena. Thus forces of nature appear the same way in all their countless phenomena. These forces manifesting in terms of causality are also called 'laws of nature'. It is their conformity and subservience to the laws of nature that gives the entities in the lower grades of the will's objectification a different character from that of the higher grades. The lower entities of nature are predictable, strictly subject to the laws of nature, and devoid of individual character in contrast to the human beings. Schopenhauer says that he is simply tracing the implications of Kant's great insight that space, time and causality do not belong to the thing-in-itself. These apply only to the phenomena (W-I, 134).

Thus we should realize that explanation from causes can go only so far. It must stop at a point; otherwise, we will end up reducing the content of all phenomena to their form and nothing more than form. Schopenhauer also mentions that to posit the ground of all things in the original forces is a mark of a thinker's indolence. These original forces are not the ultimate ground of the phenomena. 'They don't constitute the total force, any more than a hammer and anvil constitute a blacksmith' (W-I, 142). To appeal to the objectification of the will is not to be a substitute for discovering a physical explanation. To appeal to the creative powers of God is also a mark of intellectual indolence, wherein one stops short of tracing the ultimate ground of the phenomena which appears to us through the principle of sufficient reason. Schopenhauer concludes that 'Philosophy everywhere and in nature also considers the universal alone. Here the original forces themselves are its object, and it recognizes in them the different grades of the objectification of the will that is the inner nature, the in-itself of this world' (W-I, 141).

Schopenhauer cautions that the presence of the same will in all Ideas as original forces does not mean identity of these ideas themselves. For example, chemical or electrical attraction cannot be reduced to gravitational attraction. One force cannot be posited higher or more perfect than the others, just as in reference to species, we cannot call the more perfect as a variation of the less perfect. The distinctness of the individual Ideas as well as the forces of nature has to be recognized, even though the will is their mutual ground.

WILL, STRIFE AND KNOWLEDGE

The strife, struggle and contest for supremacy is visible everywhere in nature. Schopenhauer attributes it to the will's essential variance with itself. It seems that all grades of will's objectification strive for and contest the same matter, space and time. Matter constantly changes form, and organic phenomena seem to snatch the matter from each other. Animal kingdom is full of mutual conflict. Animals feed on the plant life or prey on other animals. It seems that will-to-live feeds on itself; it is its own nourishment. When we arrive at the human race, it asserts its supremacy over all of nature and 'regards nature as manufactured for its own use'. But the will's variance with itself is very much present within humanity. We witness among humans a terrible conflict and contests for supremacy, and the statement *homo homini lupus est* (man is a wolf for man), the oft-quoted adage by Schopenhauer, has some truth in it. We have to recognize that 'universal conflict is essential to the phenomena of the will.'

In the forces of nature as well, conflict is a necessary feature. The forces of attraction and repulsion as those of gravitation and rigidity penetrate the will's objectivity at its lowest grade. At the lowest grade of inorganic nature, the will is a blind impulse or a dull urge, and a striving far from possessing any knowledge. It appears this way in all the original forces. The aim of physical sciences is to become familiar with their laws. Schopenhauer points out that the will objectifies itself as an 'obscure driving force' devoid of knowledge in the lower grades. In plant life, stimulus rather than knowledge is at work. The vegetative part of the animal life is also moved by stimuli. The will's objectivity ultimately reaches a higher level where mere stimuli are not sufficient for its phenomena to obtain their nourishment in a situation of overcrowding, confusion and competition. 'Thus movement consequent on motives and because of this, knowledge, here become necessary . . . for the preservation of the individual and propagation of the species' (W-I, 150). Schopenhauer maintains that every determination of the self-objectifying will is represented by an organ. Knowledge is represented by the brain. With the advent of knowledge in higher animals, especially in the case of man, world as representation comes into being with all its forms, subject, object, time, space, plurality and causality. Up to now in inorganic and vegetative nature, the world was merely will. Now it is also representation. At this higher grade of its objectification, with the endowment of knowledge, the will 'kindles a light for itself'.

'That complicated, many-sided, flexible being, man, who is extremely needy and exposed to innumerable shocks and injuries, had to be illuminated by a twofold knowledge in order to be able to exist' (W-I, 151). Man is endowed with a power of perception and reason as the faculty of forming abstract concepts. This brings into existence thoughtfulness, ability to assess future and the past, as well as deliberation, carefulness, premeditated action and awareness of the decisions of one's own will. In contrast to the strict conformity to law, and infallibility of inorganic nature, the individual's own deliberation with allied irresolution and uncertainty, confusion and error appear as features of human consciousness. Will's manifestation here is no simple process, the interplay of multiple motives, which can be falsely interpreted or become delusionary and driven by superstition as imaginary motive, all impact on the course of the manifestation of man's will.

Schopenhauer emphasizes that knowledge is always subordinate to the will, for it comes into being to serve the special purposes and needs of the highest grade of will's objectification, merely as an expedient to fulfil the aim of the will to preserve and procreate this higher species. 'Therefore, destined originally to serve the will for the achievement of its aims, knowledge remains almost throughout entirely subordinate to its service' (W-I, 152). However, in rare cases, in some thoughtful and determined individuals, who recognize the machination of the will, knowledge is able to 'throw off its yoke' and begin to live a life of the denial of the will-to-live. The fuller details of this practice will be examined in a subsequent chapter.

'To think is to confine yourself to a single thought'[1] says Heidegger.[2] That single thought for Schopenhauer is the thought regarding the will. Hence he strives to fathom the will on every page of his writings. He continues to explore the nature, the pervasiveness and enigmatic operations of the will within all the themes of his philosophy at every juncture of his philosophical journey.

CHAPTER FOUR

SUFFERING AND POINTLESSNESS

Human suffering is a constant theme in Schopenhauer's writings. Its origin, forms, nature and omnipresence in existence is a subject that his philosophy seeks to elucidate as a genuine philosophical problem. It is well known that Schopenhauer is a pessimist. His works show us that he is admittedly and proudly so, someone who regards optimism as, 'not merely an absurd but also a really wicked, way of thinking' (W-I, 326). Although Schopenhauer clearly has a dark streak in his outlook, it would be simplistic to attribute his pessimism to his personal propensities, as is often done by many of his biographers. For he does offer a cogent set of arguments for pessimism along with a substantive critique of scholarly optimistic doctrines as well as of a naïve singing of the assumed glories of human life. It is also to be noticed that the source of his arguments is not just peculiar philosophical insights but also a deeper moral standpoint on human exploitation and cruelty especially that of his times. He shows a deep empathy for victimized classes, such as black slaves, child labourers, prisoners, and those maimed and killed in wars. Add to that his deepest sympathy for the animal kingdom, a study of which he finds indispensable for a genuine philosophy of existence. At the same time, Schopenhauer frequently refers to the vanity, that is, the futility and pointlessness of human existence. Is this just an extreme standpoint of his pessimistic outlook on reality or does he have genuine philosophical insight underneath his radical judgement of the ultimate value of human life as such?

SUFFERING AND THE WILL-TO-LIVE

Endless human desires and striving for their fulfilment, and frequent hindrances and failures in the way of this striving, are all traced by

Schopenhauer as the very nature of the will-to-live. The will which is the innermost nature of life, seduces man to affirm it constantly and yet is never satisfied.

> At all grades of its phenomenon, from lowest to the highest, the will disposes entirely with an ultimate aim and object. It always strives, because striving is its sole nature, to which no attained goal can put an end. Such striving is therefore incapable of final satisfaction. (W-I, 308)

According to Schopenhauer, human being is a phenomenon of the will, just as other entities are, at all grades of Being, inanimate things, plants and animals also are. The will is always goal oriented and has aims which it is striving to accomplish incessantly in all levels of its phenomenon. Everything is striving to realize its nature. Since will brings aims, goals and dynamism to all things, it fills them with endless striving. Thus man is a bundle of needs, wants and cravings which know no final satisfaction, unless the will at the summit of its knowledge of itself, in the human existence alone, resolves to deny rather than affirm itself. Striving is the kernel and in-itself of everything that exists which in case of human existence, manifests itself most distinctly being endowed with a human consciousness superior to that of all other entities. This striving in man is appropriately called 'will', by Schopenhauer a term indicative of resolve, process, goals, ends and endless desires. When the will is hindered through obstacles between it and its temporary (immediate) goal, it is called 'suffering'. Thus suffering is defined as hindrances placed in the advance of the will towards its immediate and presumed aims. The attainment of the temporary goal of the will is defined as satisfaction, well-being, and happiness by Schopenhauer. Thus both suffering and temporary satisfaction do not deliver lasting happiness, since each so-called satisfaction is the starting point of a new striving. 'Thus that there is no ultimate aim of striving means that there is no measure or end of suffering' (W-I, 309). Thus inevitability of striving that is part and parcel of the will means that suffering is inevitable and ineradicable as a matter of course. This gives Schopenhauer the rationale for his pessimistic judgement of life as such.

Schopenhauer offers a graphic account of suffering in human life throughout his early and later writings. Suffering is felt to the highest degree in human existence because in human existence, knowledge is

ever more distinct than in any animal and in its enhanced consciousness, pain also increases. Schopenhauer asserts that the more one
knows the more one suffers; a genius suffers most of all. Although
suffering is more feebly expressed in animal world, it offers a mirror
to the human to witness how 'all life is suffering', for life means 'striving' and striving never has a smooth sailing.

Life is also a constant warding-off of death, 'a prevented dying,
an ever deferred death'. Knowing that there is death, struggling to
nourish and preserve the body is another reason for suffering. Thus
the will is more appropriately named 'will-to-live'. Willing and striving are the essence of all living and the basis of willing is need, lack
and hence pain. In case of the highest grade of will's objectification,
the human body appears as an objectified will-to-live, with an iron
command to nourish it. Thus man is a bundle of needs and wants.
An additional task in-built in this concretized will-to-live is to propa-
gate the species. As Schopenhauer explains in his essay on sexual
love, the purposes of the will-to-live are unknowingly carried out by
those attached in the bond of love and marriage. Furthermore, the
needs and wants of romantic love have their own aspects of suffering.

Furthermore, when objects and activities of willing are temporarily missing, boredom strikes and existence seems to become a burden.
'Hence life swings like a pendulum to and fro between pain and boredom' (W-I, 312). Ensuring and striving after their own existence is
what keeps all living things engrossed and in motion at all times. As
soon as their existence is ensured to human beings or striving after
existence gets a respite, they are at a loss as to 'how to kill time' this
becomes a big issue. Being free of existential cares at once makes
humans burdens to themselves. Boredom is not to be taken lightly
for it imposes a compulsory sociability on people and obliges them
to seek out one another, even though at bottom due to deep-seated
egoism, there is no love lost among them. At the same time, human
life is a continuous surge between willing and attainment. But the
satisfactions of petty attainments are short-lived and wishes appear
under new versions and forms. Schopenhauer acknowledges that
pure knowledge and genuine delight in art transforms us to being
pure spectators of existence. But since pure intellectual and aesthetic
pleasure require rare talent, they appear in very few. And these select
few receive this higher satisfaction at the cost of feeling very lonely
among beings that are incapable of pure knowledge and aesthetic
feeling. These moments of pure knowledge and art-experience are

also like fleeting dreams in an existence that is given over to willing and craving for the most part.

It is the accidental nature of the appearance of sufferings that accords them their power. Suffering is essential to life and it is really its various forms that make their appearances subject to chance. But we frequently overlook the basic fact that 'suffering is essential to life, therefore does not flow in upon us from outside, but everyone carries around within himself its perennial source' (W-I, 318). Thus all satisfaction or so-called happiness is only negative. Every satisfaction is fulfilment of a wish, and a wish or lack or desire has to be the precedent condition of every pleasure. Schopenhauer returns to the theme of the positive nature of suffering in all of his early and later works. He is quick to point out the moral failings of human egoism in his graphic description of human miseries. How the sight or description of another's sufferings brings us a feeling of satisfaction is described by Schopenhauer with a quote from Lucretius: 'Not that it pleases us to watch another being tormented, but that it is a joy to us to observe evils from which we ourselves are free' (W-I, 320). An evidence of Schopenhauer's observation can be found in the reactions of the tourists to the plight of the poorer native populations around the sun and sand destinations. Many tourists seem to draw a perverse feeling of joy at their own superior economic situation and can hardly suppress their self-congratulatory satisfaction during their bouts of eating and drinking in their all-inclusive resorts.

As if the cares, anxieties and preoccupations of the actual world are not enough, human mind has a tendency to create an imaginary higher world for itself, a world of demons, gods and saints and a thousand superstitions. To these conceived deities must be offered 'sacrifices, prayer, temple decorations, vows and their fulfilment, pilgrimages, salutations, adornment of images and so on'. Events of this life are accepted as the counter-effects of these divine beings. Such religious activities fulfil a double need of people for help and support as well as for activity and diversion. Schopenhauer points out that such spiritual and religious innovation took place more significantly among peoples whose lives were made easy by mildness of climate and fertility of soil, first among the Hindus, then Greeks and Romans and later Italians, Spaniards and others.

Schopenhauer emphasizes that his account of life's suffering is not just an 'a-posteriori' accumulation of instances of human miseries within history and experience. This could be deemed as a one-sided description lacking in universality which is required in a philosophical analysis. He maintains that his account is a 'perfectly cold and philosophical demonstration of the inevitable suffering at the very foundation of the nature of life; for it starts from the universal and is conducted a priori' (W-I, 324). However, an a-posteriori confirmation of this truth is to be found everywhere. What Schopenhauer means is that the reality and primacy of human suffering is not merely deduced from the various instances of pain and rejection in human condition. Rather, suffering lies at the core of life as real and inevitable, part and parcel of existence as such. All the instances of suffering which seem to be accidental occurrences are rather essential and inevitable components of existence, a testimony to the truth of suffering residing in the core of life. Of course, there are innumerable satisfactions felt at the realizations of the goals of our strivings. But these are short-lived and too few compared to the widespread frustrations at the thwarting of the will's endless cravings that prompt ceaseless quests. Add to these frustrations of wilful projects of human being, the tragic facts of the nature of existence, needs, wants and necessities of the basic demands of life, the knowledge that death is certain but its timing is uncertain, the pains of human relationships, meetings and partings. All in all, the nature of life and its many-coloured unfoldings contain an ocean of suffering. A significant part of it is lawful and inevitable aspect of existence itself, another part is bound to subdue us even though there is a portion of it that we can possibly encounter and overcome with heroism. Schopenhauer maintains that a happy life is impossible; a heroic life of compassion and fortitude is an option.

According to Schopenhauer, anyone whose judgement is not paralysed by prejudices of assured optimistic doctrines will acknowledge that 'this world of humanity is the kingdom of chance and error'. Folly and wickedness are rampant in it. Schopenhauer continues to present a graphic account of the darker aspects of human life. In this world, everything better and excellent struggles through as an exceptional occurrence, and lasting creative works of great minds are those that have outlived the malice of their contemporaries. In the sphere of thought, art and action, the absurd, the dull and the fraudulent are the order of the day, disturbed only by brief interruptions of the contributions of the genuine heroes and genius intellects. As far as the individuals are concerned, 'as a rule, every life is a continual series of mishaps great and small, concealed as much as possible by everyone' (W-I, 324). Everyone is aware that others will draw a per-verse satisfaction at the miseries of others from which they are at the moment free. How can anyone in one's right mind call this unjust and miserable world 'the best of all possible worlds' Schopenhauer wonders. If we were to take the most 'hardened and callous' optimists through hospitals, prisons, torture-chambers, slave-hovels, battle-fields and other abodes of misery, they would have to give up their doctrines of the glories of human existence.

But this hopeless and irreversible condition of man is 'precisely the invincible and indomitable nature of his will, the objectivity of which is his person' (W-I, 325). An external power can never change or sup-press this will, and no supernatural power can possibly deliver him from the sufferings that are the consequence of the life which is a phenomenon of the will. Everything depends on the individual left to himself; any possible deliverance depends on the will of man himself. In vain does he make gods for himself, and seeks from them through prayer and flattery what can be brought about only by his own will-power. As man does have the capacity to deny this will-to-live as exemplified by *sanyasis* (monks), martyrs and saints of all faiths. But optimism, at a fundamental level as the basic judgement of the nature of life, remains a 'bitter mockery of the unspeakable sufferings of mankind'. Schopenhauer shows the atheistic tenor of his thought and offers a scathing critique of ritualistic religion. However, he shows a great deal of admiration for saints and ascetics of all major religions, for he views them as genuine practitioners of the denial of the will, a difficult but nobler way of life.

The acknowledgement of the suffering inherent in human life is the starting point of wisdom and higher life according to Schopenhauer. He regards this pessimism as realism. To overlook and downplay the misery of others is both insensitive and immoral; to deny suffering in one's own life shows shallow thinking. Suffering is very real and continuous throughout life's various phases and at the same time delivered to us in totally unpredictable and staggering modes, and changing realities are hard to handle. The respites from suffering, happy interludes are far too few and short-lived. By no means are suffering and happiness equal and opposite. Suffering is fundamen-tal; the will and its allied cravings ensure inevitable hardship. All hap-pinesses and satisfactions are temporary breaks from the ongoing suffering essential to life. This is certainly a pessimistic and one-sided appraisal of life based on an interpretation of the character of the will-to-live, both willing and living being ongoing quests and ongoing strivings, involving innumerable goals and innumerable frustrations. Due to the fact that our bodies and our lives are the abodes and arenas of the will-to-live, life and suffering have to be synonymous as two sides of the same coin. The evidence for this basic truth can be found everywhere in the human condition. Schopenhauer cites instances of common woes and miseries, along with the meanness of human egoism, systemic exploitation of the downtrodden and widespread heartlessness as sure signs of suffering that is part and parcel of life. Does Schopenhauer deliberately and/or compulsively downplay the positive and the good in human life? He does acknowledge the good but only in a heroic encounter with suffering, and in an impassioned contemplation of the nature of the world by a small number of thinkers, artists and geniuses, and most of all in the saintly lives of those who say 'no' to the will's commands and cravings. Any other happiness or good has to be a temporary delusion according to him. The change, the striving and movement within life is taken to be something negative, a pointless turmoil, the opposite of the calm of salvation. Thus the Buddhist dualism between *samsara* (worldliness) and *nirvana* (salvation) seems to be embedded in Schopenhauer's insight.

VANITY AND SUFFERING OF LIFE

Schopenhauer's next writing that explicitly deals with the problem of suffering appears in volume 2 of the *WWR*. This supplementary essay added to the second and expanded edition of the *WWR* has a very befitting title, namely, 'On the Vanity and Suffering of Life'. The vanity here is to be understood in the sense of pointlessness or futility. Life is both pointless and full of suffering because of its matter-of-course subservience to the will. According to Schopenhauer, love of life or the view of it as a glorious possession is erroneous, for life is, for the most part, a delusionary affirmation of will's endless cravings doomed to be thwarted by reality. What Schopenhauer wants to emphasize is that sufferings of life are neither accidental nor negative but essential and positive. Thus suffering is not a negation of matter-of-course happiness, but in fact, happiness is brief interruption of matter-of-course suffering. Thus life on the whole cannot be called good, glorious and by itself meaningful. It is something that cannot be regarded in itself a good occurrence. It is something whose denial is more important than its affirmation. Thus life as such is to be recognized as vain, pointless and futile. It does offer to an individual an opportunity for the will's denial and thus on that account human life is superior than that of an animal.

'Everything in life proclaims that earthly happiness is destined to be frustrated, or recognized as an illusion. The grounds of this lie deep in the nature of things' (W-II, 573). Schopenhauer faces the root of suffering in 'the nature of things', that is, the way will is both within and outside of us. It is not just a matter of happiness and suffering both being equally present in life, but suffering having the upper hand due to the ceaseless strivings and cravings of the will necessarily resulting in constant stresses and disappointments. Schopenhauer offers his insights into the comedy that life plays with us. Although he clearly takes the pessimistic outlook, his observations surely contain a ring of truth. 'Life presents itself as a continued deception . . . If it has promised, it does not keep its word, unless to show us how little desirable the desired object was' (W-II, 573). Happiness seems to lie either in the future or in the past. The present is like a 'dark cloud over a sunny plain' constantly moving and casting a shadow. The present is sold out to the hopes for the future or to the fond memories, biased in favour of assumed happy interludes from the past. The vanity of all objects of the will and ceaseless exertion to chase them makes life 'a business that does not cover its costs'. 'We feel pain, but not painlessness; care, but not freedom from care; fear, but not safety and security . . . only pain and want can be felt positively . . . well being, on the contrary is merely negative' (W-II, 575). Schopenhauer points out that humans are scarcely conscious of the three greatest blessings of life, namely, health, youth and freedom as long as they possess them. We become aware of them when we lose them. Pain is felt more intensely than pleasure. Therefore pain is positive. Happiness and pleasure pass by relatively unnoticed; thus they are a negation of pain. 'We become conscious of time when we are bored, not when we are amused . . . our existence is happiest when we perceive it least; from this it follows that it would be better not to have it' (W-II, 575).

Such statements of Schopenhauer regarding existence, that is, 'it would be better not to have it' have puzzled many scholars and readers of his works. This outlook that *nirvana* is preferable to the world or the voluntary giving up of the life of will's subservience is preferable to the thoughtless and obsessive involvement with wilful and petty goals of life, or simply put, the denial of the will is preferable to the affirmation of the will, shows Schopenhauer's appreciation of Buddhism. It would be better not to have life is not said in the sense of a recommendation for suicide. It means that life as it delivers itself to us, as a thoughtless slavery to the will's ceaseless cravings, is inferior to the life that denies the will as far as possible. The same insight is contained in Socrates' profound saying: it is not living that counts, but living well. It would be better not to have life as it comes; it must be encountered with a resounding 'no' to its will-to-live.

To debate whether good exceeds evil in the world or vice versa is ultimately futile, asserts Schopenhauer. Mere existence of the evil is decisive, since evil can never be eliminated or counterbalanced by good. The existence of evil is fundamentally unacceptable to the human mind; it has always provoked philosophical inquiry and poetic lamentations. Schopenhauer sprinkles his essay with numerous quotes from classical and modern writers and poets with respect to the unsatisfactoriness of this world. At the same time, he makes such radical judgements about the undesirability of existence as such, which are very difficult to understand or to swallow by many of his critics. For example, he maintains that 'we have not to be pleased but rather sorry about the existence of the world; that its non-existence would be preferable to its existence; that it is something which at bottom ought not to be' (W-II, 576). Schopenhauer's radical standpoint shows his pessimistic interpretation of the Vedanta (Hindu) and Buddhist thought-systems which regard coming into the world or more precisely, being caught up in the worldly-cycle (*samsara*) as well as in the illusory worldliness (*maya*) and cravings (*trishna*) as undesirable for a higher life destined for salvation (*moksha* or *nirvana*). The impact of these Eastern systems is quite incontrovertible on Schopenhauer, even though he claims that he thoroughly studied these sources only after the publication of the first edition of *WWR*, and merely found a re-authentication of his ideas in Eastern thought. We must keep in mind that Vedanta and Buddhism cannot be called pessimistic in themselves because they attach great importance to human life being a glorious opportunity to expiate the baggage of bad karma and to lead a moral life (dharma) on the way to salvation (*nirvana*). It is quite obvious that whereas Schopenhauer pays highest tribute to the Eastern systems by incorporating them into Western philosophy in general and his own philosophy in particular, he does use or abuse them for authenticating his own ideas. At the same time, he finds numerous Western classical and modern sources which seem to echo his radically pessimistic outlook. All this is done by creatively mingling the 'nature of the world', 'coming into the world' and 'leading an immoderately worldly life' under the general concept of the world, much like what concept of the *samsara* is supposed to convey in Vedantic and Buddhist thought-systems.

Schopenhauer outlines a scathing critique of the conduct of human entity towards its own kind. Although it is characteristically pessimistic and negative portrayal of human nature, it cannot be called untrue. 'The chief source of the most serious evils affecting man is man himself. Man is a wolf for man (*homo homini lupus est*)' (W-II, 578) Schopenhauer gives the example of the so-called conquerors and calls them 'archfiends'. These world conquerors of history, Hitler is an obvious example, set hundreds of thousand men against each other and seemed to have said to them 'To suffer and die is your destiny; now shoot one another with musket and cannon and they did do so' (W-II, 578). Besides condemning the stupidity and futility of warfare, Schopenhauer gives the examples of the slavery of blacks, and child-labour being practised in his times as instances of man's 'boundless egoism . . . even wickedness'. At the same time, man's heartlessness towards its own kind at an individual level is graphically described by him: 'In general, the conduct of men toward one another is characterized as a rule by injustice, extreme unfairness, hardness and even cruelty; an opposite conduct appears only by way of exception. The necessity for state and legislation rests on this fact, and not on your shifts and evasions' (W-II, 578). It is obviously an extreme characterization of human nature to say that it is as a rule bad and any goodness is just an exception. However, human apathy towards others and widespread egoism in inter-personal relations is well known to all of us.

Schopenhauer points towards the fact that the origin, nature and Being of the world has been a long standing philosophical problem. If the Being of the world were not a problem, it would be taken as self-evident; its totality will arouse no astonishment, its purpose would be clear-cut and inquiry about it would not arise in our minds. But it is not so. The world's Being is an 'insolvable problem' or a perennial problem within philosophy; even the most perfect philosophy will provide only a partial answer and will necessarily have an unexplained element regarding this issue. Schopenhauer believes that the will-to-live as thing-in-itself, which is not subject to the principle of sufficient reason, is the groundless principle of world's existence and fully in accord with the ultimate inexplicability of the world's Being. It also explains the unsatisfactoriness of the world. For 'only a blind, not a seeing, will could put itself in the position in which we find ourselves' (W-II, 579). This means that we are the victims of our own gullible subservience to the cravings aroused by the will-to-live. It is like the blind leading the blind. We are the blind worshippers of a blind will.

Schopenhauer maintains that we are mistaken in calling human existence a gift. It is rather a contracted debt in the form of 'urgent needs, tormenting desires, and endless misery'. The entire lifetime is spent in paying off the interest on this debt. The repayment of this loan is death, a loan which was contracted at one's birth in this world. The influence of karma theory of Hinduism and Buddhism on this interpretation of human existence by Schopenhauer is unmistakable. Accordingly, he also affirms: 'every great pain . . . states what we deserve, for it could not come if we did not deserve it' (W-II, 580).

'The capacity to feel pain increases with knowledge.' Thus no animal can feel pain as much as man. The degree of pain becomes higher in accord with the degree of one's intelligence. No human can feel pain like a genius does. Dostoyevsky, in his autobiographical novel *The House of the Dead*, illustrates Schopenhauer's point. Dostoyevsky's own pain during his confinement in a Siberian prison was much more deeply felt than many of his fellow inmates who with a peasant background seemed to be free from intellectual pain accompanying the hard labour in that prison camp.

Schopenhauer applauds David Hume's critiques of religion, and particularly those of the optimistic doctrines in his *Dialogues Concerning Natural Religion*. But he takes Leibniz to task for being the founder of systematic optimism. In reaction to Leibniz's assertion that this is the best of all possible worlds, Schopenhauer offers his contention that ours is the worst of all possible worlds, because anything even slightly worse, could not have actually existed. The conditions for a reasonably comfortable living exist so scantily and sparingly in this world. 'Nine-tenths of mankind live in constant conflict with want, always balancing themselves with difficulty and effort on the brink of destruction' (W-II, 584).

Schopenhauer calls optimism a false and pernicious doctrine due to its misrepresentation of life as a desirable mode of being and happiness as its aim. Such a doctrine encourages one to believe that one has a claim to happiness and pleasures. If, as it is usually the case, this happiness does not come about, the individual believes that he has suffered an injustice. In fact, this line of thinking misses the whole point of human existence. 'It is far more correct to regard work, privation, misery, and suffering, crowned by death, as the aim and object of our life . . . since it is these that lead to the denial of the will-to-live' (W-II, 584). Within parentheses, Schopenhauer attributes this pessimistic view to Brahmanism, Buddhism and genuine Christianity. This might be a convenient over-simplification on the part of Schopenhauer. These religions obviously do not advocate worldly-mindedness and hedonism. But they do not call suffering crowned by death as the aim and object of our life. Schopenhauer ends this supplementary essay on the vanity and suffering of life with the remark that if he were to record the comments of great thinkers of all ages on the issue of suffering, there would be no end to the citations. Thus he supplies only a short sampling of such quotes.

MORE ON VANITY

Schopenhauer returns to his favourite theme of the ultimate undesirability of life and that of suffering in chapters 11 and 12 of *Parerga and Paralipomena*, a book for popular readership which brought him long-awaited popularity and celebrity status in the twilight of his life. In chapter 11, entitled 'Additional Remarks on the Doctrine of the Vanity of Existence', Schopenhauer reflects on the nature of human existence on the whole and spells out some dreadful facts about it, the facts we all are aware of but often dismiss due to the bitterness of their truth. For we wish to cling to some sort of optimism as a convenient policy. Thus Schopenhauer enumerates some such fundamental features of life which make it on the whole a futile process which diminish its overall value. He endeavours to bring home the realization that it is important to break out of the love of life and its assumed joys, glories and gifts, and to acknowledge its overall worthlessness so that a voluntary denial of the will, that penetrates life's 'many coloured puppet-show', is embraced by an authentic human being. Such a one who voluntarily gives up the illusory pleasure of life to fully acknowledge the sufferings and injustices all around him, takes the rightly moral standpoint and path of true compassion for all living and suffering things. But a denier of the will-to-live needs to recognize the truly negative features of life which is wrongly presented to us as a bed of roses by folks with an optimistic bent of mind.

First of all, there is the finite nature of the individual is in contrast to the infinite nature of space and time. This basic finitude of human existence, makes the present moment, which itself is in passing, the only reality available to us. It gives rise to 'dependence and relativity of all things'. Here Schopenhauer seems to echo the doctrine of mutual co-arising (*pratitya samutpada*) of Buddhism. The finitude also means constant becoming without being and at a typically human level, 'constant desire without satisfaction' as well as the vanity of all striving to subserve the will in our matter of course life (PP-II, 283).

The brevity and fleeting nature of the passing moments within life and of the life itself, makes one indecisive on whether to call the enjoyment of the present moment 'the greatest wisdom' or 'the greatest folly', for to value and deem the present as real does make sense on the one hand. But on the other hand, to value temporary and doomed pleasures is like wasting serious efforts on dreams. 'Everyone . . . strives for an alleged happiness that is rarely attained, and even then only to disappoint him . . . Everyone ultimately reaches port with masts and rigging gone' (PP-II, 284). At the same time, happiness or unhappiness of an individual life which will be too soon over and finished, may be a moot question. Furthermore, there is endless but ultimately meaningless activity within life just to keep it going. A lot of turmoil and restlessness is produced by two simple urges, hunger and the sexual impulse and also by boredom. These can be called the prime movers of 'the many coloured puppet show' of human world. Thus 'constant need, ever-recurring want and endless trouble' are the stuff life is made of. In addition, every satisfaction creates a fresh desire and life's cravings, eternally insatiable, go on forever.

For most people, life remains a task of making a living. As soon as the problem of livelihood is solved, warding-off of boredom shows itself as another task. It assails every life that has been made secure from want. Schopenhauer refers to boredom again and again in his writings for he finds it a philosophically significant phenomenon in human life. Here in chapter 11 of *Parerga and Paralipomena*, he cites boredom as an evidence for the fundamental undesirableness of existence as such. This undesirability and worthlessness of existence that he keeps referring to has been puzzling for his readers and interpreters alike. If existence is worthless there is a good justification to end it. Or else Schopenhauer's thinking is absurdly and rabidly pessimistic.

If we guard ourselves against such simplistic judgements we will notice that Schopenhauer's real conclusion about the need-laden, struggle-filled, hard existence of humans, which offers only a few brief respites of painlessness, and these interludes sure to be abandoned to boredom, is that it is an existence that is by itself and at bottom, not to be valued. It is a statement which is in accord with Socrates' assertion that it is not living but living well that is to be valued. It is an attitude which may be pessimistic at first sight but upon reflection brings home the insight that being in love with life means being loaded with self-love and being obsessed with selfish pursuits of bodily comforts. This love of life which is a blind adoration of the will-to-live, stems from the notion that life itself and life as such has an ultimate value. What Schopenhauer tries to show is that this wishful and sugar-coated assumption does not pass the test of experience. The facts of human life in general and an individual's career in particular lead to the assumption that existence as such is both pointless, worthless and at bottom, empty. This is also the rightly philosophical and moral standpoint, for it alone will produce a denial of the will and a life of compassion. It truly recognizes sufferings of the others as one's own, as a worthwhile path. Singing glories of life is both a philosophical violation of truth and a moral degeneration of the first order. Schopenhauer sums it up very expressively:

> That human existence must be a kind of error, is sufficiently clear from the simple observation that man is a concretion of needs and wants. Their satisfaction is hard to attain and yet affords him nothing but a painless state in which he is still abandoned to boredom. This then, is a positive proof that, in itself, existence has no value, for boredom is just that feeling of its emptiness. (PP-II, 287)

Thus boredom is a manifestation of the 'worthlessness and vanity' of existence which dawns upon us whenever there is a respite from striving. The same boredom appears in the form of a pomp and splendour of the rich. Their luxury and amusements are nothing but a pathetic attempt to overcome the essential wretchedness of human existence. 'For after all, what are precious stones, pearls, feathers, red velvet, many candles, dancers, putting on and off of masks and so on?' (PP-II, 288)

MORE ON SUFFERING

After reflecting on the vanity, that is, the futility or pointlessness or emptiness of human existence as such at a fundamental level, Schopenhauer returns to his favourite theme of the sufferings contained within human existence in chapter 12. It is entitled 'Additional Remarks on the Doctrine of the Suffering of the World'. The issue of suffering, on which most other philosophers are either unclear or silent, is very much a central doctrine in Schopenhauer's philosophy. Suffering (*dukkha*) happens to be the starting point or main impetus for philosophical inquiry in Buddhism. Although Schopenhauer's reading of Buddhism is characteristically too pessimistic, the impact of this Eastern system is quite visible in his works. This chapter written for the non-academic as well as the academic, summarizes Schopenhauer's previous writings on suffering and at the same time offers some additional remarks, that is, some additional insights from our day to day lives, some additional embellishments through his powerful writing style.

Schopenhauer begins with the remark that omnipresent suffering must have to do with the basic reason of life, since it is absurd to assume that infinite pain is just purposeless and accidental. Although each fact of misfortune seems to be an exception, according to our usual approach to instances of suffering, it must be recognized that 'misfortune in general is the rule'. At the same time, Schopenhauer emphasizes, as he did in previous writings, the positive nature of pain, that is, well-being should be considered as nothing positive but merely the absence of pain. For example, in our personal experience we do not notice the general health as well-being of our whole body, but only 'where the shoe pinches'. It shows that instances of minor pains, annoyances and unwelcome trifles are more deeply felt than our overall blessings or sporadic strokes of happiness.

It is absurd, says Schopenhauer, to take evil as negative and then to produce theodicies, or philosophical justifications for evil, as thinkers like St Augustine and Leibniz have done. The undesirable aspects of the nature of the world are very real. Schopenhauer gives us a remarkable mixture of realism with pessimism, when he says that history depicts the life of nations mostly in terms of wars and insurrections, brief periods of peace appearing only here and there. Similarly, the life of an individual is a perpetual struggle with want and boredom as well as with rivals of all kind. 'Everywhere he finds an opponent, lives in constant conflict, and dies, weapon in hand' (PP-II, 292).

It seems that human life won't be itself, without the constant 'care, anxiety, pain and trouble'. If all desires were fulfilled instantly how would people occupy themselves? If in an Utopia, 'everything grew automatically and pigeons flew about already roasted; where everyone at once found his sweetheart and had no difficulty keeping her; then people would die of boredom or hang themselves' (PP-II, 293). The way we are, we don't seem to deserve any other kind of existence. Schopenhauer continues his critique of egoism and selfish indulgences of the human entity. In seeking enhanced pleasures, humans deliberately increase their basic needs. Hence their use of 'delicacies, tobacco, opium, alcoholic liquors, pomp, display' etc. Add to that a source of pleasure peculiar to man, namely, honour and shame, that is, his care for other people's opinion of him. Finally, for man the instinct of sexual satisfaction invariably transforms into an obstinate selection of a definite individual of the other sex. And this is bound to make his or her life even more complicated and full of additional challenges. The inner nature of the love between the sexes is discussed in a remarkable detail by Schopenhauer in volume 2 of *WWR*. Of no less importance is the fact that to the human entity alone, its certain but unpredictable death is actually known, and this terrible truth is forever looming in its mind.

The pain suffered by man is greatly enhanced in contrast to that of animals due to his faculty of reason and reflectiveness. Human reasoning and knowledge makes susceptibility to pain attain its highest point on the one hand, and may bring the subject to the possibility of denying the will, on the other. Thus the existence of pain in human life is not purposeless. It may serve as a catalyst for the higher possibility of one's comprehension of the pointlessness of the worldly cravings produced by the over-active will-to-live, and making a resolve to live a life of the denial of that will. Thus according to Schopenhauer the suffering in life is real, well-deserved and a catalyst towards a higher life of asceticism. The law of karma and the life of dharma as the doctrines of Buddhism and Vedanta seem to reflect themselves in a peculiarly pessimistic form in Schopenhauer's thought. In fact, Schopenhauer applauds Hinduism and Buddhism for their critical stance of the world (*samsara*), that is, having come into Being is a kind of original sin (due to the weight of bad karma). He also finds the ancient Greek doctrine of world and gods being the work of a necessity, and the Zoroastrian account of the conflict between Ormuzd and Ahriman, as also quite reasonable. 'But that a Jehovah creates this world of misery and affliction . . . and then applauds himself . . . this is something intolerable' (PP-II, 301). Schopenhauer finds Old Testament Christianity as having no convincing doctrine of the origin of the world and takes it to task for being the only religion that has no doctrine of immortality or reincarnation. However, he finds the allegory of the fall of man quite conducive to his own theory.

Schopenhauer maintains that in genuine Christianity, that is, the New Testament version, human existence is quite correctly considered a 'the consequence of guilt, a false step'. Accordingly we should not regard the sufferings and troubles in this world either unexpected or abnormal. We should rather find such things as quite normal for 'here everyone is punished for his existence and indeed each in his own way' (PP-II, 303). Such an outlook will enable us to accept 'the wretched and contemptible nature of most men, both morally and intellectually'. Schopenhauer shows an elitist attitude in his condemnation of the intellectually and morally inferior mankind which includes most of humanity except a handful of geniuses and morally superior natures. The world is an arena of suffering and unjust exploitation of others. 'This world is just a hell and in it human beings are the tortured souls on the one hand, and the devils on the other' (PP-II, 300). This is indeed a bleak and deeply pessimistic view of the common conduct of humanity and seems to have a complete disregard of the notion that there is something basically good in every individual, a soul or a conscience. But Schopenhauer's extreme pronouncements never fail to be thought provoking.

CHAPTER FIVE

AESTHETICS AND THE ARTS

The reflections on aesthetics and individual fine arts occupy almost one-fourth of Schopenhauer's chief work *WWR*. In his later works, numerous essays are devoted to art and art forms. Human preoccupation with art is deemed to have epistemological and redeeming qualities that provide glimpses of the deeper being of things as well as perspectives on a salvation from the misery-laden worldliness created by the will's striving. According to Schopenhauer, an authentic delving into art enables the human entity to know its world as it is through an objective observation and contemplation. An encounter with art is also a momentary experience of freedom from the demanding and oppressive will-to-live. Art, therefore, can be an impetus for human beings to live a life of voluntary denial of the will-to-live, a higher way of life according to Schopenhauer.

Art experience is a momentary suspension of the will which enables the artist to contemplate Ideas of things in their purity. The recognition of the will-to-live and its manifold implications, including the uniquely human possibility of breaking free from the will's oppressive regime and stepping on to the road of salvation and voluntary denial of the will are shown to have an intimate connection with the creation and experience of art in Schopenhauer's system. Besides producing a temporary will-lessness, art experience makes possible a contemplative apprehension of Ideas. In his artwork, the artist reproduces or 'repeats' his original apprehension of Ideas. The Ideas, that is, the Platonic Ideas, are the 'immediate and adequate objectivity of the thing-in-itself, or the will'.

IDEAS AS THE OBJECTS OF ART

The will objectifies itself as Ideas (i.e. Platonic Ideas) and as human representation at different grades of its objectification. Schopenhauer calls the Idea as the immediate and therefore, 'most adequate' objectivity of the thing-in-itself, thus tracing a connection between Platonic Idea and Kant's thing-in-itself. 'Only . . . the eternal Ideas, the original forms of all things, can be described as truly existing, since they always are but never become and never pass away' (W-I, 171). The specific things appear in accordance with the principle of sufficient reason to the human mind. Particular things are comprehended as part of the world as representation in terms of their interconnection with each other, and seldom in isolation as individual entities standing in themselves. The particular thing perceived in terms of the principle of sufficient reason is merely an indirect objectification of the will. Between this particular thing and thing-in-itself (will) stands a more direct objectivity of the will, that is, the Ideas. Being a higher objectivity than the merely causal and conceptual objectivity within space and time under the principle of sufficient reason the Idea is described as the 'most adequate objectivity' by Schopenhauer. 'As a rule knowledge remains subordinate to the service of the will . . . in fact, it sprang from the will . . . as the head from the trunk. With the animals, this subjection . . . can never be eliminated. With human beings, such elimination appears only as an exception' (W-I, 177).

Among human beings, transition from the common knowledge of particular things to knowledge of the Ideas happens suddenly in the mind of a rare individual, a genius or a great artist endowed with such ability. In such a subject, knowledge tears itself apart from the service of the will, as he ceases to be a mere individual and becomes a pure will-less subject of knowledge. When this power of the mind is aroused, the forms of the principle of sufficient reason no longer guide the subject whose will is suspended and he 'no longer considers the where, the when, the why and the whether in things, but simply and solely, the what' (W-I, 178). It is as if one loses oneself in the object; the difference between the perceiver and the perceived is no longer felt and the entire consciousness is pervaded by a single image of perception. What is known in this mode is not an entity as such but the Idea, the eternal form by a 'will-less, painless, timeless, subject of knowledge'. When the Idea arises, 'subject and object reciprocally fill and penetrate each other completely.' Schopenhauer follows Plato's theory of Ideas in terms of the relation between things subject to change, the phenomena and the eternal forms and deems it essentially alive in Kant's concept of thing-in-itself. He creatively applies this theory in the domain of aesthetics:

> Now what kind of knowledge it is that considers what continues to exist outside and independently of all relations . . . and is therefore known with equal truth for all time, in a word, the Ideas . . . It is art, the work of genius. It repeats the eternal ideas apprehended through pure contemplation . . . According to the material in which it repeats, it is sculpture, painting, poetry or music. (W-I, 184)

According to Schopenhauer, human life under the subjection of the will is for the most part full of striving and suffering interspersed with brief interludes of satisfactions of trivial achievements which result in pursuits of newer and newer worldly goals. But art experience is something that pulls one out of the matter of course oscillation between suffering and illusory satisfaction. In a contemplation of an object (or a specific set of objects) free from its ties with other objects, that is, in contemplation if its Idea, a detachment is achieved by the artist and passed on to the art connoisseur. Schopenhauer maintains that in this mode of detachment, art experience leads one to a state of will-lessness or a self-transformation as well as endows one with a truly objective knowledge of the Ideas of things. One becomes a pure will-less subject of knowledge as one gains a truly objective knowledge. These moments of art experience, as long as they last, usher one to a state of liberation from the network of worldly interconnections of things, a network which is consumed with personal agendas, temporary satisfactions leading to newer lacks and newer sufferings. In art experience one's personal stakes and agendas to manipulate and use things is temporarily suspended and one is able to stare at the thing itself to contemplate its Idea. According to Schopenhauer, art experience brings both an extraordinary knowledge and an extraordinary self-transformation. It gives us intimations of what a life of the denial of the will and salvation referred to in great religions like Christianity, Hinduism and Buddhism must be like.

ART AS THE WORK OF A GENIUS

Schopenhauer maintains that great art is produced by a genius. Great art is not produced by merely talented or trained individuals but a genius who alone is capable of pure contemplation of Ideas. A genius is pre-eminently able to detach himself from his personality and personal considerations, and to absorb himself entirely in the object. 'The gift of genius is nothing but the most complete objectivity' (W-I, 185). Genius is the ability and tendency to remain in a state of perception, to immerse oneself in perception and to remove one's knowledge from the matter-of-course service to the will. According to Schopenhauer, a genius has a superfluity of knowledge in contrast to other mortals, an amount of knowledge that far exceeds what is normally required for the service of an individual will. The knowledge of the Ideas contemplated by the genius is obtained through an especially keen perception. It is not abstract or conceptual knowledge. The perception of a genius is more penetrating in contrast to the typical perception of an ordinary man who can 'direct his attention to things only in so far as they have some relation to his will . . . he does not linger long over the mere perception . . . quickly looks merely for the concept under which it is to be brought, just as the lazy man looks for a chair, which then no longer interests him' (W-I, 187). On the other hand, the genius is often so absorbed in contemplation of life itself and Ideas of things that he is invariably forgetful of his self-interest and lacks in practical life skills that the ordinary man of the world possesses. The issue of the genius was of great interest to Schopenhauer as he paints portraits of the genius in several of his works. One of the themes he dwells over is the connection between genius and madness.

The genius is one who has the capacity of bypassing in his sight worldly inter-connections of things, that is, the mundane knowledge according to the principle of sufficient reason, in order to focus on the thing as such to discover its Idea. He is able to grasp the real inner nature of a thing and how that thing represents its whole species. At the same time the genius has the power to be a 'correlative of the Idea'. That is, he becomes a 'pure subject of knowing', and ceases to be an individual in the mode of contemplation. 'That which exists in the actual individual thing, only imperfectly and weakened by modifications, is enhanced to perfection, to the Idea of it, by the method of contemplation used by the genius' (W-I, 194). This is why the perceptions of the genius artists seem extreme and exaggerated to ordinary people. 'Therefore he everywhere sees extremes, and on this account his own actions tend to extremes. He does not know how to strike the mean' (W-I, 194).

The ability of being correlative to the Ideas of things must be inherent in all, albeit in lesser degree, otherwise they would be incapable of enjoying artworks produced by genius artists. All human beings must have a power to recognize Ideas in things and must be capable of rising above their personality and personal agendas, to enjoy the aesthetic feeling for a few moments. The genius is the one who far exceeds ordinary people in dwelling in contemplation and appreciating the Ideas. The artist is endowed with the ability of repeating what he discovers about the being (Ideas) of things, in a voluntary and intentionally contrived work. According to Schopenhauer, the artwork is this 'repetition' through which the artist communicates the Idea he has grasped. Thus 'the Idea comes to us more easily from the work of art than from nature and from reality . . . The artist lets us peer into the world through his eyes . . . (His) is the gift of genius and is inborn; but that he is able to lend us this gift, is acquired and is the technical side of art' (W-I, 195).

ART AND THE GLIMPSES OF WILL-LESSNESS

Normally, human consciousness is pervaded by the will and assailed by a throng of desires with allied hopes and fears, and it can never have any prolonged peace of happiness. Schopenhauer echoes the Buddhist doctrine that craving (*trishna*) is the root cause of pain (*dukkha*) inherent in human condition. But the moments of aesthetic experience offer a temporary respite from the tyranny of ongoing willing, craving and neediness. These moments are enjoyed by the creative artist as well as the people who authentically experience artworks. These moments offer aesthetic pleasure as well as an extraordinary objective knowledge of things. It is a glimpse of salvation which must be a state of will-lessness.

When, however, an external cause or inward disposition suddenly raises us out of the endless stream of willing, and snatches knowledge from the thralldom of will, the attention is now no longer directed to the motives of willing, but comprehends things free from their relation to the will. Thus it considers things without interest, without subjectivity, purely objectively. (W-I, 196)

Being free from willing a state of peace and painlessness arrives. The moments in which one enjoys the being or the performance of a work of art, the deliverance of knowledge from an oppressive and demanding will produces such a joy that one has a magical feeling. It is as if one has stepped into another world which is to say that one has stepped out of this familiar world. Schopenhauer remarks that 'Happiness and unhappiness have vanished; we are no longer the individual; that is forgotten; we are only pure subject of knowledge. We are only one eye of the world which looks out from all knowing creatures, but which in man alone can be wholly free from serving the will' (W-I, 198). It is interesting that in ancient Buddhist sutras, the Buddha is often described as 'the eye of the world' due to his detached and dispassionate analysis of the nature of things spelled out in the four noble truths.

According to Schopenhauer, art experience enables us to step out of the familiar world of desires and frustrations, projects and pragmata and behold the Being (Ideas) of things, and look at our own being in the world in the face. Schopenhauer points out that the essences of entities, usually hidden underneath the pragmatic network of meanings, reveal themselves in the artwork creatively brought to the fore by the genius artist. Art gives mundaneness an extraordinary twist that in its magical moments, the will loosens its grip and the world is shaken out of its foundation. The serenity of pure contemplation opens within the observer of art the power of objective knowledge free of personal obsessions. Art experience opens the gateway to the reality and value of a will-less life, which in its ideal form is called salvation. In his book *Art Experience*, the contemporary Indian philosopher, Hiriyanna, in his exposition of Vedanta theories of art seems to echo Schopenhauer's view of art:

The aesthetic attitude stands higher than that of common everyday life, which is generally characterized by personal interests . . . It is for this reason that Indian philosophers, especially Vedantins . . . compare the experience of art with that of the Ideal state . . . as *moksha* (salvation). But the two experiences are only of the same order and not identical . . . Art experience is (merely) transient, . . . seductive . . . and induced from outside.[1]

According to Schopenhauer, aesthetic contemplation is not confined to just man-made artworks. The great objects of nature too produce a feeling of the sublime. In encountering a magnificent spectacle of nature we become subjects of pure knowing, and our intimacy with Being of all things reveals itself. Natural objects of great spatial magnitude, and great antiquity, such as vast prairies of North America, high mountains, immense cliffs, rushing, roaming masses of water, complete deserts all arouse a feeling of the sublime. 'Against such a ghost of our own nothingness . . . there arises the immediate consciousness that all these worlds exist'. One gets a feeling of belonging essentially to the Being of all that exists, as the obsession with one's individuality is suppressed by a realization of one's own nothingness against the mighty and powerful manifestations of nature. Schopenhauer explains the outcomes of the feeling of the sublime, with a quote from the Upanishads: 'I am this creation collectively, and besides me there exists no other Being' (W-I, 206).

In addition to reflecting on art and the artist in general, Schopenhauer examines the natures and scopes of various fine arts, and shows his comprehensive knowledge of prominent art forms. He thoroughly analyses their ranges of activities and offers original aesthetic theories with respect to architecture, horticulture, historical painting, sculpture, allegory, poetry, drama and finally music. Schopenhauer's interest in the arts was not just theoretical but he was deeply involved in various art forms. His writings on aesthetics and the arts constitute a sizable portion of his total output. Besides devoting the entire Third Book of volume I of the *WWR* to aesthetics, he added numerous supplementary essays in volume II to aesthetics and individual fine arts. In volume II of *Parerga and Paralipomena*, several essays are devoted to topics such as beauty, aesthetics, authorship, language, literature, architecture and music. In his personal life marked by loneliness and frustrating relationships with people around him, Schopenhauer always found a solace in the pursuit of the arts. He was a regular visitor to the opera and dramatic performances and to art museums. During his travels, art appreciation was an important part of his itinerary. He had a deep interest in observing objects of plant life and believed strongly that a keen observation of animal kingdom was a must for any serious investigation of life and philosophy. He was a fine scholar of classical languages and literature. His flute playing in the mornings as a daily ritual indicates his personal involvement with music.

His account of individual art forms applying his theory of aesthetics that revolves around the apprehension of the Ideas as well as a will-less knowing is both original and insightful. He begins with a synopsis of architecture, along with some references to hydraulics and horticulture, and then offers a thorough account of historical painting and sculpture. Finally, he reflects on allegory and poetry and more extensively on music. It won't be an exaggeration to say that more than one-fourth of his writings are devoted to aesthetics, arts and related matters. The reason for his deep involvement with art is not hard to guess. The suffering and pointlessness of life can only find solace and substantive remedy in the heroic practice of will-lessness. Art is a mirror to the eternal Ideas behind phenomenal entities of the world and the hazards of endless cravings aroused by the will's ceaseless strivings. Schopenhauer shows us that art is a catalyst for will-less knowing and becoming a pure subject bereft of one's personal stakes in life. Art is an impetus to live the life of a denial of the will to live. Hence, the persistent and life long interest of this thinker in aesthetics and the arts.

In his hierarchy and classification of the arts in accordance with their subject-matter, Schopenhauer closely approximates the Platonic hierarchy of the Ideas, the lowest being those of inorganic natural matter. Higher than these grades of will's objectification are plant life, and still higher is the animal world. At the summit of the objectification of the will is humanity and the human world. Thus architecture deals with the lowest Ideas or the weakest objectivity of the will such as 'gravity, cohesion, rigidity, fluidity, reaction to light and so on' (W-I, 214). Horticulture and paintings of nature are concerned with somewhat higher grades of ideas pertaining to plant life. Drama and poetry are the arts dealing with the highest Ideas of humanity, character and actions of human beings. Although Platonic Ideas are the cornerstone of Schopenhauer's aesthetics, he does not accept Plato's view that individual things rather than the Ideas are the prototype of painting and poetry (*Republic*, X-601), nor does he share Plato's disdain and rejection of art (W-I, 212). For Schopenhauer, Ideas alone are the object of a genius artist, and art is most important for discerning reality and true purpose of life. Art is most important for knowing and living.

Before we move on to a brief consideration of Schopenhauer's exposition of the major art forms, one more thing is to be kept in mind. In art creation as well as art appreciation, the two dimensions of Schopenhauer's theory of aesthetics, namely the apprehension of the Ideas and the will-less knowing of the pure subject do not happen equally and to the same extent in each and every art form. Rather, in different arts, different degrees of the subjective element, that is, the will-less knowing will appear. In arts dealing with lower grades of will's objectivity and lower Ideas of inorganic and vegetative nature, such as architecture and horticulture, apprehension and enjoyment of will-less knowing is predominant. In the arts wherein animals and human beings and their humanity are the objects of aesthetic contemplation, the objective apprehension of the Ideas is more prominent and more sophisticated aspects of the revelation of the nature of the will. Historical painting and drama fall into the category of arts in which the objective element of the knowledge of the higher Ideas and the more comprehensive picture of details and meanings of the phenomena of the will are grasped. Thus although both the knowledge of the Ideas and the experience of will-lessness are present in all art forms, they are present in different proportion in different fields of art. Let us now briefly consider how Schopenhauer applies his theory of art to individual arts.

ARCHITECTURE

Architecture seems to be a manipulation of material stuff. Apparently, the qualities of matter are the subject-matter of aesthetic contemplation. These qualities are the phenomena of Ideas, even though matter as such cannot be the expression of an idea. Schopenhauer remarks that Plato was right in designating matter as something neither an idea nor an individual thing (*Timaeus*, 48–9). The most universal qualities of matter are 'gravity, cohesion, rigidity, fluidity, reaction to light and so on' (W-I, 214). These ideas are also the weakest objectivity of the will.

Architecture can be a fine art even though it serves the will in creating useful entities such as buildings, etc. As a fine art it performs the function of highlighting some of the Ideas pertaining to the qualities of matter which are at the lowest grades of will's objectivity such as gravity, cohesion, rigidity, hardness, etc. These are the visible qualities of stone, 'the simplest, dullest visibilities of the will, the fundamental bass-notes of nature'. According to Schopenhauer, the simple aesthetic material of architecture is the conflict between gravity and rigidity. Architecture aims at making this conflict appear distinctly in many creative ways. For example, a building presses on to the earth due to gravity whereas with various devices of architecture rigidity, which is also an objectivity of the will resists the gravity and thwarts its tendencies by letting it happen only indirectly, for example, by letting the joist, beams and arches press on to the earth by means of columns and square pillars. To show by enforced digressions and deliberate hindrances, the interplay between rigidity and gravity is the fundamental aesthetic purpose of architecture. Since these forces of gravity and rigidity are best reflected in stone, other building materials such as wood, pumice-stone or other artificial substances fail to show real architectural achievement. According to Schopenhauer, what addresses us through architecture is not symmetry or ornamentation, which is something borrowed from sculpture, but the interplay between the fundamental forces of nature, that is, rigidity and gravity, the primary Ideas at the lowest grades of will's objectivity. These are the least subtle and most visible and basic forms of the will. Symmetry and ornamentation please the eye, but these are not the principal things in architecture. 'Even ruins are still beautiful.'

The works of architecture also have a special consideration for light, because the variety and illumination of light reveal the interplay between rigidity and gravity, distinctly and creatively. At the same time the nature and beauty of light itself, appears more distinctly in reaction the work of architecture. Schopenhauer's theory regarding architecture is illustrated by the famous building Taj Mahal, although he does not cite this example. The beauty of the Taj lies in the highest quality of the marble stone and the solidity of its structure that seems to oppose the force of gravity in a unique way. The impact of light on this beautiful building, which is more a work of art than a mere mausoleum, is a wonderful spectacle. In the haze of the morning, in the full sunshine of the afternoon, in the twilight and in the moonlit night, transparent marble structure appears in different colours, in manifold forms of beauty. This is why an art critic called it 'a poem in marble'. In the examples given by Schopenhauer, he contrasts buildings erected in the mild climates of India, Egypt, Greece and Rome with buildings from northern Europe where the necessities of a harsh climate required coffers, pointed roofs and towers. In his essay on architecture in volume II of *WWR* Schopenhauer contrasts Gothic architecture which borrows too much from sculpture, with ancient architecture of Greece marked by its ability to present the primary conflict between solid mass and gravity.

Architecture differs from other arts insofar as in it the art is invariably subordinated to practical ends. Because of the largeness of its structure and the costs involved, architectural works are produced by professionals supported by society. The art achievement of the architects lies in how he or she makes the architectural beauty of a temple, a palace, a prison or an office building compatible with its functionality. The only sister art of architecture seems to be artistic arrangement of water, where the idea of lucidity, mobility and transparency appear as distinctly as rigidity and gravity do in architecture. However, this art is seldom combined with practical hydraulics in the same way as art and utility are combined in architecture.

HORTICULTURE, LANDSCAPE AND ANIMAL PAINTING OR SCULPTURE

Moving one step upwards in the next realm of ideas, we have artistic horticulture. Although landscape beauty depends on the nature's objects present in it, the artistic horticulture achieves clearer separation, association and succession of these objects. This art is not a master of its material just as architecture is, and is helpless against inclemency of weather. Schopenhauer does not distinguish between non-representational and representational art, as he arranges the arts in accordance with the hierarchy of Ideas. Since the cornerstones of his aesthetics are the emergence of the Ideas as well as the will-free knowledge, arts are not arranged according to their materials but according to the kinds of Ideas they depict. Thus, according to Schopenhauer, along with horticulture, landscape painting too depicts the plant world. In painting of still life, architectural works, ruins, church interiors, etc. the subjective, that is, will-free knowledge aspect is predominant, not as much the manifestation of Ideas as such. But in landscape paintings, which depict vegetation and nature, Ideas depicted are more suggestive, the aesthetic experience is more balanced between Ideas and pure knowledge. A still higher grade of will's objectivity is revealed in animal paintings and animal sculpture. In these the objective aspect prevails over the subjective aspect of aesthetic experience. Knowledge of these Ideas of the animal species is accompanied by a peace of the silencing of the spectator's will. But the full impact of this peace is not felt because human beings share the same will with animals, and the animal's restlessness and monstrosity disturbs the peace of the art experience. Yet the animal appears in its originality, freedom and innocence because their will unlike human will is not controlled by thoughtfulness. This is what explains human interest in animal kingdom.

HISTORICAL PAINTING AND SCULPTURE

These arts deal with the highest grade of Ideas, in which the will attains the highest degree of objectification, namely, the presentation for perception the aspects of humanity. Schopenhauer points out that in case of any manifestation of the human being in an artwork, the character of the species has to be presented alongside the character of the individual human subject. In case of animal painting or sculpture, the character of the species alone is the problem for the artist, and not the character of the individuality of the animal. Thus historical painting and sculpture deal with a complex combination of Ideas. The objective apprehension of the Ideas or pleasure in the beauty is more predominant in historical painting and sculpture whereas the subjective reaction is less pronounced. Schopenhauer calls *beauty* as something that has to do with the Idea of the species, and *character* as something that concerns the Idea of the individuality of the individual. The artist of historical painting has to present both beauty and character in the same individual. The knowledge of the beauty, that is, the Idea of the perfections of the species is not something that the artist learns by experience, but as a genius he has the a-priori ability to anticipate the perfect aspects of the species. In the true genius, the anticipation of the Idea is 'accompanied by . . . a recognizing in the individual thing, its Idea . . . understands nature's half-spoken words . . . He impresses on the hard marble the beauty of the form which nature failed to achieve in a thousand attempts' (W-I, 222). In presenting the peculiar character of the individual alongside the perfect attributes of the species to which the individual belongs, the painters and sculptors depict the individual's being not as an oddity or an accidental appearance of a peculiar entity, but 'as a side of the Idea of mankind, specially appearing in this particular individual' (W-I, 222). In other words, the artist presents a masterful combination the general humanity and a particular manifestation of the Idea of humanity, which is itself an Idea, and not just a quality of the general Idea of the species. Since 'the individual always belongs to humanity . . . and humanity always reveals itself in the individual, . . . therefore, beauty cannot be abolished by character, or character by beauty' (W-I, 225). This creative combination of a particular world of a particular people with the worldhood of the human world in general is the hallmark of a great work of art, maintains Heidegger in his 'The Origin of the Work of Art'.[2] In his own terminology, Heidegger seems to echo Schopenhauer's insights into the nature of the world and the depiction of that world in the great specimens of art such as historical painting. 'To fit the fleeting world which is forever transforming itself, in the enduring picture of particular events that nevertheless represent the whole, is an achievement of the art of painting' (W-I, 231).

According to Schopenhauer, historical painting reaches its acme in the works in which the real ethical spirit of Christianity is revealed in the depiction of persons in full possession of this spirit, usually a group of saints along with Christ, often as a child with his mother and angels. The great masters of this art form are Raphael and Correggio. These paintings are most expressive because they reflect not only the highest objectification of the will in depicting true humanity but also the denial of the will on the part of the spiritual beings shown in such paintings. Their eyes show most perfect knowledge of Ideas and the inner nature of the world and of human life. 'The perfect resignation which is the innermost spirit of Christianity as of Indian wisdom, the giving up of all willing . . . the abolition of the will . . . and hence, salvation' (W-I, 233).

POETRY

The basic aim of poetry is to reveal Ideas and to communicate them to the reader. The medium in which the Ideas are made to be perceived by the reader with the power of the reader's own imagination are the concepts. The abstract concepts which are the direct material of poetry are transmitted through the words of the poet which sculpt the reader's representation and imagination towards the perception of the Idea. Schopenhauer points out that the range of Ideas that poetry communicates is the widest; it is not confined to a limited grade of will's objectification as architecture or animal sculpture are. Plastic and pictorial arts may surpass poetry in the presentation of the lower grades of will's objectification, that is, in inanimate matter or plant and animal life, because these subjects may reveal their inner being in their outer forms in a static moment. Man's Being on the other hand, is a much more complex issue, which is captured by poetry in a network of human actions, thoughts and emotions, through a dynamic approach. Poetry is able to capture progress and movement of its objects in a manner that the plastic and pictorial arts cannot.

Schopenhauer maintains that 'far more real, genuine, inner truth is to be attributed to poetry than to history' (W-I, 245). The historian focuses on the significant actions with historical consequences and influence of powerful characters, and bypasses the significant actions of distinguished individuals such as writers, artists and reformers who are not political power players. 'The poet, however, apprehends the Idea, the inner being of mankind outside all relation and all time' (W-I, 245). Thus poetry is closer to truth in capturing time-less being of man whereas the historian is caught up in transitory and ulti-mately trivial upheavals. According to Schopenhauer, some classical historians are borderline poets when they rise above the historical data and unfold human nature in their portrayals of the Idea of man-kind. However, the hands of the historian are never free of historical facts and this is why the works of the great classical poets offer a truer and clearer picture of man's inner essence.

Schopenhauer does not find history as the most accurate study of man's inner nature. He gives a greater value to biographies and particularly to autobiographies than to history proper. In these stud-ies of the lives of actual human beings, the data of human life are put together more accurately and more completely, whereas history proper seldom considers real humanity as over and above nations and armies, pomp and circumstances. Schopenhauer disregards the critique that autobiographies are usually full of exaggerations and dissimulation. Biographies and especially autobiographies are closer to truth because they show 'the conduct of men in all its nuances and forms, the excellence, the virtue, and even the holiness of individuals, the perversity, meanness and malice of most, the profligacy of many' (W-I, 247) as they intersect a single life. This idea of Schopenhauer that biography and autobiography can be the best medium and method of philosophizing, was discussed and emulated in European hermeneutics. Wilhelm Dilthey (1833–1911) captures life-world-experiences (*Erlebnisse*) and lived-worlds (*Lebenswelt*) of several thinkers and wrote their biographies, maintaining that composing a biography was the best way of doing philosophy.

Schopenhauer discusses the various forms of poetry and the way they reveal Ideas. In lyric poetry, the depicter and the depicted can be the same, when the poet describes his own subjective state. In other forms of poetry, the depicter may conceal himself entirely. In the ballad, the subjective is still present, which diminishes in the Idyll, still more in the romance, almost entirely in the epic. In the drama, which according to Schopenhauer is the most objective, most comprehensive and most difficult form of poetry, there is no vestige of the subjective.

In romance, epic and drama, which are the more objective forms of poetry, the Idea of mankind is unfolded by the presentation of important characters and in the creation of remarkable situations in which the characters show their personality. According to Schopenhauer, tragedy must be placed at the summit of poetic art, due to the greatness of its impact and the difficulty of its authorship. Tragedy reveals the real nature of the world and of human existence, which is marked by real and unsurpassable misery, unremitting pursuit of the will and almost sure barrage of frustrations resulting from thoughtless subservience of the will. Why Schopenhauer regards tragedy as the most accurate and powerful art form is graphically spelled out in his excellent prose:

> The unspeakable pain, the wretchedness and misery of mankind, the triumph of wickedness, the scornful mastery of chance, and the irretrievable fall of the just and the innocent are here presented to us; and here is to be found a significant hint as to the nature of the world of existence. It is the antagonism of the will with itself which is here most completely unfolded at the highest grade of its objectivity, and which comes into fearful prominence. (W-I, 253)

At the same time, tragedy reveals the reaction of certain thoughtful characters to the misery of life, in their ability to see through the veil of *maya*, egoism and false individuality. As they relinquish the motives of the will, the true knowledge of the real nature of the world dawns upon them and serves as a quieter of their will, produces resignation and renunciation. Schopenhauer cites some famous tragedies of European literature which show the final resignation by their main characters, for example, The Prince of Calderon, Gretchen in the *Faust* and by Hamlet. Schopenhauer takes Samuel Johnson to task for critiquing *Hamlet* for lack of poetic justice, and thereby showing a lack of understanding of the nature of tragedy. Real tragedy has no poetic justice. When we wonder what wrong have Ophelias,

Desdemonas and Cordelias have done, we misunderstand what tragedy really conveys, namely, the true nature of life which is unjust and full of undeserved pain. Often not just the wicked but also good people are cruel to others. Good people at times end up inflicting pain on others without intending any harm.

According to Schopenhauer, the presentation of great misfortune, essential to tragedy, is achieved by the poet in one or more of the following three ways: (a) through extraordinary wickedness of a character (e.g. Othello, Shylock, Iago); (b) through blind fate, chance or error (e.g. Oedipus, Romeo and Juliet); (c) through the very attitude of the persons to one another in the web of human relations (e.g. Hamlet, Faust). According to Schopenhauer, it is the third kind of tragedy that is really excellent in showing the true nature of life. Here 'the characters . . . are so situated with regard to one another that their position forces them, knowingly, and with their eyes open, to do one another the greatest injury, without any of them being entirely in the wrong' (W-I, 255). In this kind of tragedy, life itself makes these characters to act out the real nature of life, that is, unfair and replete with unwanted but regularly unfolding suffering. Hamlet's heartlessness towards Ophelia and Othello's cruelty towards Desdemona are the examples of the harshness of life and circumstances.

MUSIC

Music stands apart from all the other arts insofar as it does not stimulate or present the knowledge of Ideas. According to Schopenhauer, the power of music lies in its unique imitation of the inner nature of the world, in its being a copy of the will itself rather than being a copy of the Ideas. Ideas constitute the adequate objectivity of the will and are the subject-matter of all the other arts except music. Music is the only art that imitates and transmits the nature of the will without the medium of the Ideas. Schopenhauer reflects on the power and the impact of music on human beings. 'It is such a great and exceedingly fine art, its effect on man's innermost nature is so powerful, and it is so completely and profoundly understood by him in his innermost being as an entirely universal language' (W-I, 256). Furthermore, music which everyone can instantly relate to and understand, seems to have a certain infallibility due to the fact it has definite rules and an inner connection with numbers, which cannot be violated if it is to be music proper. Schopenhauer says that after a deep reflection on the different forms of music, he arrived at 'an explanation of the inner essence of music and its imitative relation to the world' (W-I, 257). This explanation is obviously grounded on Schopenhauer's all important concept of the will.

All the arts other than music stimulate the knowledge of the Ideas by depicting specific and remarkable 'things' as works of art, and they bring about this knowledge of the Ideas to the connoisseur by transforming him or her into a pure subject of knowing that overcomes his or her individuality. In other words, the artist lends his own eyes to the connoisseur to witness the Ideas in a thing called the work of art. Heidegger seems to offer a similar account of the artwork in his 'The Origin of the Work of Art',[3] albeit in his own non-metaphysical terminology. Although Heidegger is silent on the role of Platonic Ideas in art, he begins his essay by reflecting on the thinghood of art works and mentions that art works are after all things first and foremost. Just as Schopenhauer, Heidegger emphasizes the self-transformation in the connoisseur and the fact that the connoisseur must become a 'preserver' of the art work by being bereft of the worldly assumptions of his or her own times. Heidegger also seems to agree with Schopenhauer that the purpose of art is to offer a disclosure of the worldhood of the world.

According to Schopenhauer, music is unique among fine arts insofar as it does not offer a specific thing or object as a work of art. It offers a knowledge of the worldhood of the world in another manner. Music is independent of the phenomenal world. The phenomena are the 'appearance of the Ideas through plurality through entrance into the *principium individuationis*, the form of knowledge possible to the individual' (W-I, 257). Unlike the other arts, music is 'as immediate an objectification and a copy of the whole will as the world itself is'. This is why the impact of music on the humans is more powerful, penetrating, and universal than any other art. Other arts speak only of the shadows (Ideas, phenomena) whereas music speaks of the essence (will, Being, world).

Just as Ideas of things have various grades such as inanimate nature, plant life, animal life and humanity, which together reflect the nature of the phenomenal world, musical harmony too expresses the concomitance of these species albeit in a non-phenomenal manner. According to Schopenhauer, the lowest grade of will's objectification, that is, the inorganic matter is represented by the ground-bass in a harmony. In between the bass and the leading voice, the ripienos producing the harmony, the various grades of the will's objectification, namely, inorganic nature, and animal world are represented. In the melody, in the singing voice that leads the whole harmony, and is a complete whole in itself, represents that highest grade of will's objectification that is the life of the human mind, the intellectual endeavours of man, according to Schopenhauer. Whatever we place under the notion of feeling, that which is not strictly covered by the abstractions of reason comes alive in melody. Schopenhauer cites Plato and Aristotle to back up his claim that melody represents the finest feelings and states of the soul (W-I, 260). Plato says that movement of the melody imitates the passions of the soul (*Laws*, VIII, 812 c). Aristotle remarks that melody, even though it is mere sound, represents the states of the soul (*Problemata*, c 19).

But from Schopenhauer's point of view, the most remarkable thing about melody as well as about music in general is that it expresses the different forms of will's efforts, especially suffering that is inherent in the will's endless strivings as well as brief satisfactions followed by more striving. Will's temporary satisfaction is indicated by harmonious interval and returns to the keynote. The adagios represent great and noble human quests. The composition of a melody that exposes the deepest levels of human willing, feelings and emotions is the work of a genius. The composer reveals a copy of the will in a language that his reasoning faculty does not understand. It is a spontaneous creation without the aid of concepts. However, 'In the composer, more than in any other artist, man is entirely separate and distinct from the artist' (W-I, 260). In music, the composer overcomes his own individuality, in being a subject of pure knowing, and creating music through inspiration and spontaneity. This is how this artist builds his composition to present a copy of the inner movements of the will. A great musician offers an objective rather than a subjective picture of the will. 'Music does not express this or that particular or definite pleasure, this or that affliction, pain, sorrow, horror, gaiety, merriment or peace of mind, but joy, pain, sorrow, horror, gaiety, merriment, peace of mind themselves. . . .' (W-I, 161). Schopenhauer's thoughts on the fine art of music are comparable to the classical Indian theories of art, specifically the theories of *rasa* (sentiments), for example in Bharata's *Natyasastra*, which mentions eight fundamental sentiments or emotions (*rasas*) as objects of art, namely, exotic, comic, pathetic, furious, heroic, terrible, odious and marvellous. In the words of Hiriyanna, the *rasa* theory shows that 'art aims rather at inducting in us a unique attitude of mind which signifies not only pleasure, but also complete disinterestedness and a sympathetic insight into the whole situation.'[4] Thus music as an art exposes not a specific or subjective sorrow, horror and gaiety but gives us a taste of what sorrow, horror and gaiety are like in their essences as part and parcel of the will to live. 'Music gives the innermost kernel preceding all form, or heart of things' (W-I, 263). Because music shuns all conceptualizations and rational network of meanings to get at the heart of things, we feel an immediate affinity with it but neither the composer, nor the listener can explain it in concepts. 'The inexpressible depth of all music, by virtue of it floats past us as a paradise quite familiar and yet eternally remote, and is so easy to understand and yet so inexplicable' (W-I, 264). Because emotions or up and down swings of the will are its subject matter, music cannot offer rational or conceptual exposition of elusive but deeply felt emotions. It reproduces the will's upswings and downswings in a way that we can immediately relate to, but cannot fully explain.

CHAPTER SIX

THE ENIGMA OF LOVE

By reflecting on the nature of love between man and woman, Schopenhauer claims to cover an uncharted territory on the part of philosophers. Although a few philosophers including Plato, Rousseau, Kant and Spinoza have touched on the mystery of love, their treatments have been limited and shallow according to Schopenhauer. Plato's account seems to concern 'only the Greek love of boys', Rousseau's is 'false and inadequate', Kant's 'without special knowledge' and Spinoza's, amusing due to its 'excessive naivety'. Thus Schopenhauer exclaims: 'I have no predecessors either to make use of or refute' (W-II, 533) on this issue. However, one is amazed to witness the overwhelming preoccupation of poets and novelists, especially the writers of romances, with the subject of love between the sexes. We must acknowledge that love must be very consistent with human nature since it has been so consistently described by poets and novelists and accepted by their readers with undiminished interest. The passion of love does not merely exist among the characters of fictional works, but newspapers often inform us about many a lover ending their lives when their chances of uniting with their partners seemed hopelessly thwarted. Many more end up in the madhouse as victims of the same passion. Thus one must wonder why 'a matter that plays so important a part in the life of man has hitherto been almost entirely disregarded by philosophers' (W-II, 532).

Schopenhauer believes that the basic doctrines of his own system hold a key to the resolution of the enigma of love between the sexes. He hopes to bridge a gap in the history of philosophy by presenting a philosophical account of the force that seems to take over the minds of the individuals involved and unbeknown to lovers themselves, the project of a higher life force gets underway through them.

Schopenhauer apologizes in the beginning of his exposition that his description may seem 'too physical, too material' to the lovers under the sway of this passion.

Schopenhauer begins his essay with a very definitive statement about the nature of love. 'All amorousness is rooted in the sexual impulse alone, is in fact . . . specialized and . . . individualized sexual impulse, however ethereally it may deport itself' (W-II, 533). Love is often understood as something beyond mere sexual attraction, even as entirely asexual in forms known as Platonic love, higher love, meeting of souls, etc. But Schopenhauer asserts very strongly that all romantic love is sexual, no matter how much this truth is covered up or given transcendental interpretation by the lovers. This sexual impulse is not general but fixed towards a specific individual. Schopenhauer was one of the first thinkers in Europe to recognize the important part played by sexuality in human life and especially in the life of the mind. No wonder he was a major influence on the thought of Sigmund Freud.

The impact that the sexual love has on the individuals affected by it is simply overwhelming. Schopenhauer affirms that it is next only to the love of life itself in being one of the strongest motives that prompts far-reaching activity in the pursuit of its goals. It especially lays claim to the bulk of the thoughts and powers of the young, it jeopardizes important affairs, interrupts serious occupations, and in many cases the 'negotiations of statesmen and investigations of the learned'. This passion can damage valuable relationships, and lead to quarrels and disputes and even wars. It can alter upright characters into traitors, deceivers and practitioners of disloyalty, in many cases destroying health, wealth and happiness.

'Why all this noise and fuss? Why all the urgency, uproar, anguish and exertion? Is it merely a question of every Jack finding his Jill?' (W-II, 534). Schopenhauer believes that he can provide an explanation of the intense and overwhelming nature of love, and the rush of feelings of those in love seems to stem from a higher force. The fervour of love in the individual is indeed in keeping with the importance of the matter for the human species. According to Schopenhauer, what is decided by love is nothing shorter than the formation of the next generation. Individuals in love have the delusion that they are serving their very own interest, but in fact they are acting according to the deeper objective of the will-to-live to perpetuate itself. For the sexual impulse appearing in an individual consciousness is essentially the will-to-live. But this sexual impulse fixed towards a definite individual is the will-to-live 'as a precisely determined individual'. What Schopenhauer means is that in order to achieve its hidden purpose of bringing forth a new human being, the nature conspires to bring two individuals of the opposite sex together in amorous attraction. The affair of the hearts is a stratagem of the will-to-live to perpetuate the species and what counts in it is not the mutual affection and compatibility but 'possession', that is, physical fulfilment. This is in keeping with Schopenhauer's assertion that 'all amorousness is rooted in the sexual impulse alone'.

'The collected love-affairs of the present generation taken together are accordingly the human race's serious meditation on the composition of the future generation on which in their turn innumerable generations depend' (W-II, 534). Thus, love and falling in love has a serious purpose, often hidden from the lovers themselves. It is something necessary from the standpoint of the species that it must perpetuate itself. It does so through the natural amorous and sexual attraction between men and women and makes them couples. Two individuals of opposite sex enter into a bond of fixed attachment. Each individual in such a relationship wants a union with his or her partner and this partner alone to fulfil his or her intense desire, which is in fact, the nature's hidden purpose to produce a specific child through this and this union alone. These partners are meant for each other do a specific job for nature which only they can do, says Schopenhauer. Thus every love affair is distinct and individual, just as every individual has an individuality. Hence the anguish and frustration to be suffered by the individual when the nature's purpose fails against unfavourable worldly circumstances.

The connection between love as mutual affection and possession is highlighted by Schopenhauer. He maintains that the certainty of mutual liking and admiration can never make up for the lack of possession, that is, physical fulfilment. Forced marriages and a woman's favour purchased with gifts and even rape, indicate that possession as physical enjoyment is often considered more important than mutual affection and compatibility. 'The true end of the whole love-story, though the parties concerned are unaware of it, is that this particular child may be begotten; the method and manner . . . is of secondary importance' (W-II, 535). Thus, Schopenhauer explains why possessiveness and jealousy are natural accompaniment of romantic love. Love as mutual adoration is never enough. It must be consummated in the formation of a couple with mutual and exclusive possession. For nothing less will fulfil nature's goal, namely, the producing and nurturing of a healthy child.

What pulls two individuals of the opposite sex together so powerfully in the will-to-live that abides in the whole human species and seeks in the new individual which this couple can potentially produce, an objectification and expansion of its true nature? Thus, the will uses the lovers to realize the aim of its own continued objectification and propagation of the species. 'The quite special and individual passion of two lovers is just as inexplicable as is the quite special individuality of any person, which is exclusively peculiar to him' (W-II, 536). Thus, the mystery of and mystifying nature of love between a specific couple is ultimately inexplicable just as the individuality of an individual is ultimately inexplicable. This is because the will as the spirit of the human species is involved in both cases. A specific love affair is not just a matter of a rational and calculated decision taken by the individuals concerned. The same way the quite special character of the personality of any individual is not just a sum total of that person's experiences and rational decisions. It carries within it a uniqueness that is ultimately inexplicable and inimitable. Sometimes we name it the mystery of the self.

Schopenhauer tries to reflect on many perplexing questions concerning the nature of love between a man and a woman. What makes the bond between those involved in such a relationship stronger since not all couples seem to be equally compatible? The highest degree of the passion of love seems to be related to the suitability of the two individuals to each other. According to Schopenhauer, the child to be produced will inherit the character from the father and intellect from the mother and for this new individual, the will-to-live feels a longing. The suitability of the lovers to each other in practice amounts to a correspondence in regard to what is to be produced, since no two individuals are exactly similar. Thus, really passionate love is as rare as the meeting of two perfectly suitable individuals. But since this possibility exists in everyone's destiny, the descriptions of true love in poetic works, makes an appeal to all of us. The suitability of the lovers is defined by whether the future progeny will inherit harmonious bodily and mental qualities from the parents. Thus, one parent could supplement the looks in the other as well as complement each other's traits. Thus, a short person may choose a tall partner and a blond person may fancy a dark-haired lover. The seemingly incompatible marriages, which makes us wonder at the choices made by these individuals, may be explained by the longing of the will fulfilling its purpose of producing a harmoniously formed new being by deluding the individuals to make what seems to them, their own decisions. Thus, 'nature can attain her end only by "implanting in the individual a certain delusion", and by virtue of this, that which in truth is merely a good thing for the species, seems to him to be a good thing for himself' (W-II, 538).

Schopenhauer explains the mysteries of romantic love within the architectonics of his own metaphysics. The problem with all metaphysics is that in its project of explaining everything in a neatly crafted system, it may fall short of truth. What really makes two individuals of opposite sex strongly attracted to each other is an inner striving to subserve nature's procreative drives, according to Schopenhauer. Will-to-live, which is the name he gives to being of all beings, is a striving beyond the dichotomy of matter and form, material and spiritual, consciousness and the body, constantly needs to renew itself. Love between two mortal individuals subserves that renewal according to Schopenhauer. But is love merely a physical and sexual drive? What about devotion, loyalty, divinity, selflessness or living arrangement, partnership, family as a social unity? Schopenhauer's account does not seem to cover the ground between romantic love and love in general. However, his metaphysics does explain numerous puzzles associated with love and marriage in his own concepts and terms.

Consistent with his view of love as a feeling that subserves procreation, Schopenhauer remarks that 'by nature, man is inclined to inconstancy in love, woman to constancy' (W-II, 542). Since nature wants greatest possible increase of the species, man by nature longs for variety in sexual partners. For a man can beget numerous children in a given year, woman could have only one pregnancy in this time span. Thus man is seldom satisfied with one woman, whereas a woman clings to one man for nature urges her to hold on to the father and sustainer of the offspring. 'Accordingly, conjugal fidelity for the man is artificial, for the woman natural . . . and adultery on the part of the woman is much less pardonable' (W-II, 542). These remarks can easily be viewed as sexist and unduly exaggerating the difference between man and woman due to their biology. In fact, disloyalty on the part of women in the bonds of love and marriage is as common as that of men as some victimized men will argue. Feminist thinkers argue that women's chastity and loyalty are the vestiges of patriarchical social norms, as women were compelled to suppress their sexuality in old times of family values. On the other hand, no matter how liberated a society becomes, the differences between male and female sexuality will still remain significant and enigmatic to the extent of being inexplicable. That is why issues such as 'what a woman really wants' or 'what men are really like' will continue to be debated.

Next, Schopenhauer discusses some aesthetic and anatomical details of the factors that guide 'the pleasure in the other sex'. These may seem oddly placed in a philosophical work, but deemed by him as important to his argument. According to him, age, health, skeleton, fullness of flesh, beauty of the face are all major considerations in the arousal of the sexual attraction. For example, 'every individual loses attraction for the opposite sex to the extent that he or she is removed from the fittest period for procreation' (W-II, 543). The diseases that could pass on to the child will repel us. The figure and the shape of the skeleton, any deformities, fullness or leanness of flesh are all important considerations for prospective lovers. Most of all, beauty of the face and particularly the shape of the nose are important determinants of sexual selection. Nature and instinct play a major role in this selection and somehow proper formation of the future progeny is the main goal of the will that brings the lovers together. The rational considerations often take a back seat. Thus, 'it is a vain and ridiculous pretense when women assert that they have fallen in love with a man's mind . . . on the other hand . . . men are not determined by the woman's "qualities of character"; hence so many Socrateses have found their Xanthippes' (W-II, 545). What Schopenhauer implies is that men and women instinctively choose a partner with whom they could produce and nurture a properly formed and healthy child. Often they will go for a person who complements and supplements what they themselves have as well as what they themselves lack.

Often the considerations of whether the person chosen will make an ideal life partner or has a compatible personality are set aside and such a union makes a bad marriage. Because the procreation is the instinctive factor, both the man and the woman are guided or misled by the anatomy of the prospective partner which they scrutinize carefully and comprehensively in the process of making their selection.

Women prefer 'thirty something men at the acme of procreative power and are won mainly by man's strength and the courage connected with it', men who can beget strong children and are likely to be courageous protectors of the family. Thus, women never care for the superiority of the mind in a man, but go for manly men even if they are dim-witted and ugly. Of course, such speculation is highly one-dimensional on the part of Schopenhauer. But it seeks to explain everything about the selection of lovers and spouses, by invoking the will.

At the same time, Schopenhauer resolves some perplexing issues pertaining to relationships of lovers and married couples. Why is it that marriages based on love start so well but end up as unhappy ones? Why does the 'harmony of the souls' so quickly result in a 'howling discord'? As pointed out above, it is the suitability of the couple with respect to the being to be produced and the perfection of that being that has drawn the lovers to each other, not any 'harmony of the souls' as they might presume. According to Schopenhauer, the proper constitution and procreation of the human race is what Cupid is occupied with. Compared to the importance of this business, the details of the love stories and affairs of the individuals have no significance. However, the intensity of love between two individuals of the opposite sex increases with a high degree individualization, that is, the lovers are specifically involved with each other and it is not just a union between any man and any woman. Due to the nature's hidden purpose one partner is quite specially, the complement of the other and they find each other irreplaceable. That is why mere sexual union without regard to a special and deeper attachment, is regarded by all as 'base and ignoble', because such a union will procreate the species with respect to quantity only and not the quality. Quality is the outcome of the union between two individuals entirely suitable and complementary to each other for the purpose of producing a harmoniously constituted and healthy offspring. 'The will-to-live desires to objectify itself here in a quite particular individual that can be produced only by this father together with this mother' (W-II, 550).

On a larger canvas of reality, the will is always forming couples suitable for procreating the race. In line with the belief regarding reincarnation in Hinduism and Buddhism, Schopenhauer remarks that the conduct of love between the sexes indicates 'that an infinity of space, time and matter, and consequently an inexhaustible opportunity for return, stand open to the will-to-live' (W-II, 550). This may have influenced Nietzsche's concept of the external return of the selfsame. In longing of love, an inexhaustible subject in the works of the poets of all ages, which grips the lovers as an unearthly force against which their individuality becomes helpless, issues forth from what Schopenhauer calls the spirit of the species. The travails of separation and the sighs of lovers are indeed 'the sighs of the spirit of the species, which sees here to be won or lost, an irreplaceable means to its end, and therefore groans deeply' (W-II, 551).

The intense craving, infinite longing and deepest pain of separation in love happen because of this transcendent nature of love that does not merely attack one's individuality but the core of that individuality that is the will. In this mode the will summons the individual to subserve the cause of the species. Hence, the overwhelming attachment, jealousy, torments and pangs of separation. When a hero wails over lost love, it does not seem odd to the spectators of the drama, because 'it is not he but the species that wails' through him. The same passion of love makes one do uncharacteristic things. Honourable people of high station end up in scandals, adultery and unconscientious conduct in complete disregard of honour, duty and loyalty. It is true to say that a higher force takes possession of those in love, as the lovers often feel that worldly morality and conventions no longer apply to them. Schopenhauer offers a very profound quote from Chamfort: 'when a man and a woman have a very strong passion for each other, . . . (they) belong to each other "by nature" and by "divine right" in spite of laws and human conventions' (W-II, 553). Schopenhauer maintains that it is their service of the spirit of the species that uplifts the lovers from their seemingly narrower selfish gratification. It is due to the higher calling as well as the nobler and blameless nature of love that audiences of plays and readers of novels find themselves sympathetic to the efforts of the lovers towards their ultimate union.

Schopenhauer's view of the real source of love in something other than the intellect will be readily acceptable to all who have experienced the onslaughts of romantic love. The core of one's individuality is identified by him as the will, which has to be more powerful and based in something more than mere individuality. The will seems to identify itself with the species rather than a specific individual. While will is the ground of all self-love and all urges to live and live it up in the world, it is more than mere individuality. For it can look away from that individuality and use it as tool for its own ends. That is why, while in love, an individual feels as if he is ruled by an alien power. Whether romantic love which must have some connection with love in general, is a mere ploy of the procreative urge in us and nothing more, remains a debatable issue.

Romantic love brings out comic or strange behaviour in the affected individual, and at times it may lead to tragedy. One seems to be possessed in this state by something, which Schopenhauer identified as 'the spirit of the species'. One seems no longer one's usual self as if ruled by a transcendent inclination. The will of the person in love seems to be 'caught up in the whirlpool of the will of the species'. In extreme cases it may lead to extreme depression, madness, suicide or double suicide. Often the individual under the sway of this passion, acts against his or her own rational judgement, and ends up opting for a marriage partner entirely unsuitable and discordant. This is why we often witness 'very rational and even eminent minds' tied to 'termagants and matrimonial fiends, and cannot conceive how they could have made such a choice' (W-II, 555). The woeful matrimonial lives of Socrates, Shakespeare, Albrecht, Durer and Byron are cited by Schopenhauer. We may add to that the case of Tolstoy whose noble life was harassed by a shrew of a wife. We can be sure that many female celebrities might have faced similar fate in the age when divorce was uncommon. This certainly lends truth to the adage 'love is blind'. The reason that romantic love, often appears as a temporary episode in one's life or declines with the passage of time, or its spontaneity is transformed into a challenge for the married couples, is explained by Schopenhauer as something bound to happen after the will of the species has fulfilled its purpose. Contemporary studies on love and sex reveal that love fever is most intense in the first nine to twelve months of the courtship, which is exactly the time required for conceiving and delivering a child.

Schopenhauer believes that legendary god of love, Cupid correctly represents the genius of the species. He has been described as spiteful, cruel and notorious god with a childish appearance. He is also an impulsive and dictatorial demon. That he is the lord of gods and men is indicated by the following words of Euripides quoted by Schopenhauer: 'Eros, tyrant of gods and men' (W-II, 556). All these attributes of Cupid are exposed in the nature of love described by

Schopenhauer in his essay. There is spitefulness and cruelty in the rejection suffered by a lover as well as a childlike spontaneity. The vehemence of love has despotic hold over an individual in the grip of this passion and even gods were believed to be subjected to the darts of Cupid. That this strong feeling makes the lovers take leave of their faculty of reason is amply illustrated in Schopenhauer's account.

Since sexual love ultimately serves the interest of the species, Schopenhauer maintains that marriages based on romantic love, for the most part, do not deliver happiness and compatibility for the couple. After the passion wanes, the partners discover that they have different natures due to which they cannot get along and their initial experience of compatibility on other scores was a delusion. The obvious differences of rank, education, cultural background, financial well-being, etc., which were dismissed as unimportant in the fever of love, become real problems with the passage of time. Thus 'marriages contracted from love prove as a rule unhappy . . . He who marries from love has to live in sorrow, says the Spanish proverb' (W-II, 557). But this is not the case with marriages of convenience, that is, those based on rational considerations, including those contracted through the active involvement of the parents and families of the prospective spouses, the so-called arranged marriages. In case of such arranged marriages, the prime consideration is the well-being of the individuals rather than well-being of the species. Thus, in marriage, convenience and passionate love seldom appear together and either the interest of the species or of the individual must suffer.

Towards the end of his essay on love between the sexes, Schopenhauer retraces the connection between the metaphysics of love and his metaphysics on the whole. In other words, he wants to emphasize that the attraction between the sexes is not just a peripheral matter but a central aspect of the philosophy of human existence. Schopenhauer brings home the insight that if meditation on death is the chief task and prime mover of philosophical thinking, the connection between death and love is also a central theme of philosophy. Thus, the hitherto neglected philosophical investigation of love is undertaken by Schopenhauer in this pioneering work. The connection between love and death and between this essay on love and his philosophical system on the whole is explained by Schopenhauer as follows. Man's true being-in-itself is indestructible, as exposed in the essay on death and indestructibility of our true nature. In other words, man's being has a stake in the coming generation. This explains why the impulse of love exercises such a powerful influence on him or her. The race that follows man's current life-span cannot be entirely different from him, and he is not absolutely perishable in death. This does not mean that Schopenhauer endorses reincarnation of the individual in 'flesh and hair' in a simplistic way. He wants to emphasize that man's inner craving to live on enables him to live on in the species. 'His true being-in-itself lies rather in the species than in the individual' (W-II, 559).

As explained above, the root of all love affairs is the best possible constitution of the species. Being in love of a man and a woman demonstrates that being of the species is nearer or more real to them than his or her being as an individual. 'Why, then, does the man in love hang with complete abandon on the eyes of his chosen one? . . . Because it is his "immortal part" that longs for her' (W-II, 559). A treatise on devotional love in the Hindu tradition called *Narada Bhakti Sutra* similarly argues that love is basically a longing for immortality; it is a longing to transcend the tedium of usual worldly life of self-interest and material pursuits to peep into the immortal aspect of our existence where happiness of happiness given to another becomes more important than personal gratification. Schopenhauer expresses the same thought as follows. 'Now this is the will-to-live, and hence precisely that which has so pressing and urgent a desire for life and continuance. Accordingly, this remains immune from, and unaffected by death' (W-II, 560).

CHAPTER SEVEN

A WELCOME TO EASTERN THOUGHT

It is well known that Schopenhauer was greatly impressed with Eastern philosophies and religions from the very beginning of his academic studies. His interest in Eastern thought, especially in the Indian thought-systems of Vedanta and Buddhism, deepened with the advance of his scholarly career. It is quite obvious even from a casual perusal of his works that he was an admirer of Indian philosophy and was greatly influenced by the insights contained in the Upanishads and Buddhist texts. While some of the impacts of these Eastern philosophies on Schopenhauer's system and its doctrines are explicitly acknowledged by him, many other implicit Eastern influences and comparable assumptions and outlooks can be detected by a serious student. It would not be an exaggeration to say that a rudimentary knowledge of Vedanta and Buddhism is essential for a proper understanding of Schopenhauer's concepts. While the available secondary works on Schopenhauer's thought have done a good job of tracing the influences of Platonic and Kantian philosophies on Schopenhauer's system, there are hardly any comprehensive studies of the third major influence on his thought, namely, the Upanishadic and Buddhist systems. Schopenhauer himself identifies these three major influences on his thinking in a notation in his intellectual diary, during the writing (1814–1818) of the first volume of *WWR*: 'By the way, I admit that I do not believe that my doctrine could have ever been formulated before the Upanishads, Plato and Kant were able to cast their light simultaneously onto a human mind' (MR, XI, 459). In most of the scholarly studies of Schopenhauer's thought, this thinker's connections to Eastern thought are acknowledged, but only briefly mentioned and inadequately treated. This has often led to a gross misunderstanding of some of his important concepts such as those of eternal justice, death and the aftermath of man's essential being, the nature of life and its sufferings, etc. These misunderstandings on the part of his critics to a great extent are rooted in their lack of knowledge of even the basics of Eastern philosophy in general and Vedanta and Buddhism in particular. Many of these criticisms are expressions of bafflements with respect to Schopenhauer's seemingly radical and un-Western pronouncements on human life, suffering, death, the denial of the will-to-live, ascetic and saintly life, salvation, etc.

SCHOPENHAUER'S APPROACH TO EASTERN THOUGHT

But the issue of Schopenhauer's connections with Eastern thought is by no means simple and straight forward. Several issues related to his use of the Eastern materials need to be resolved. First, we need to appreciate his general attitude towards non-Western schools of thought. It seems to me that he was not interested in Indian philosophies in a merely casual way to sample something foreign and exotic. He was rather a trans-cultural thinker in the sense that he adopted a foreign tradition as his own by sympathizing with its universal message and insight. He freely adopted the Vedantic and Buddhist concepts within his own system, thereby showing his conviction that the philosophies of the world are one body of knowledge, and the compartmentalizations of philosophy as such into Western, Eastern, Indian, Chinese, Greek, etc. are artificial at a fundamental level. Schopenhauer was an atheistic and secular thinker who wished philosophy to steer clear of the Judeau-Christian dogmas. In this regard his was a very different approach from his contemporary, Hegel. On the other hand, Schopenhauer believed that philosophy should not be closed to the insights into reality and life offered by the major noble religions of the world. He had a high regard for the Christian, Hindu and Buddhist religious outlooks, whereas he showed a lack of sympathy with Judaism, Old Testament Christianity and Islam. He found New Testament Christianity quite compatible in its spirit with Hinduism and Buddhism, since all of these hold deep-rooted beliefs regarding the illusory and painful character of worldliness, in some sort of theories of original sin or karma, and uphold the lives of moral quest and renunciation as the highest. Schopenhauer believes that philosophy and religion have a meeting point insofar as both offer guidelines for better living and coping with inevitable sufferings of life. But the aspects of religion that shares the ground with philosophy have to be free of superstition, ritualism and dogmatism. This ground includes the insights into a simpler and pure living and morality of the highest order. Philosophy to Schopenhauer is not just a pursuit of truth but also a guide to a higher life of wisdom and compassion. It is also an application of wisdom to the problems of avoiding trivial pursuits or vulgar activities to overcome boredom and of managing the foolish, the envious and the ill-intentioned people in one's life. Schopenhauer's philosophy and compassion were certainly not lacking in worldly wisdom combined with his characteristic pessimism. In fact, he is one of very few philosophers who apply philosophy directly to the problems of day-to-day living in the world and suggest pathways to an authentic life.

Next, we must keep in mind the way Schopenhauer's intellectual involvement with Eastern philosophy reflects itself in his works. The Indian philosophies of Vedanta and Buddhism were his favourite sources for revalidating the truth and universality of his own system. He cited extensively from the texts of Indian philosophies and religions, which were gradually appearing in translation, and from a handful of scholarly accounts available in Europe. His interest in Indian philosophy was sparked by his attendance of the lectures by the famous Buddhist F. Majer (1813) in his university days. By the time he published the first edition of *WWR* (1819), Schopenhauer was quite familiar with Indian philosophies, as evident in the several citations of Eastern sources that appeared in this work. Two subsequent enlarged editions of *WWR* (1844, 1859) have even more references to Vedanta and Buddhism. He continues to explore and creatively employ Indian philosophical terminology in his later works, particularly in *On the Will in Nature* (1854) and *Parerga and Paralipomena* (1851). Schopenhauer pays a supreme homage to his love for Upanishadic thought in *Parerga and Paralipomena*, by way of praising Anquetil Duperron's Latin translation of a Persian version of the Upanishads, entitled *Oupnek'hat* (1802), which Schopenhauer kept by his bedside for many years. He remarks regarding the *Oupnek'hat:* 'with the exception of the original text it is the most profitable and sublime reading that is possible in the world; it has been the consolation of my life and will be that of my death' (PP-II, 397)

For serious scholars who wish to examine Schopenhauer's involvement with Eastern thought, the following basic issues need to be investigated. First, did Schopenhauer know the fundamentals of

Vedanta and Buddhism well enough prior to the publication of *WWR*, in order for the scholars to claim that the conception of this work is heavily influenced by Indian thought? Perhaps this claim is too extreme since Schopenhauer himself denies comprehensive knowledge of Indian thought-systems, prior to 1819, the year in which *WWR* was published. He, however, acknowledges being surprised with the 'harmony' of his thought with Buddhism subsequent to the publication of his chief work. This subsequently discovered harmony of his thought with classical Indian systems also convinced him of the truth value of his own work. Second, we must ask whether Schopenhauer's interpretation of Vedantic and Buddhist texts was fair as well as adequate even for his day and age. Can we say that he misused Indian concepts to subserve his own system? Can we claim that his interpretation of Vedanta and Buddhism was unjustifiably pessimistic to suit his own outlook and to seek revalidations of his own assumptions? These questions have often troubled those scholars who do not find Vedanta and Buddhism as fundamentally pessimistic.

SOME MISUNDERSTANDINGS OF SCHOPENHAUER'S CONCEPTS RELATED TO EASTERN THOUGHT

Some of the fundamental concepts of Schopenhauer's system remain puzzling for the interpreters of his philosophy. In the secondary literature one finds frequent bafflements and scathing criticisms of his notions of the nature of the human world, the inevitable sufferings of human life, the undesirable status of existence, the concepts of eternal justice, original sin, asceticism and the denial of the will, etc. To a large extent these hasty rejections and critiques of some of Schopenhauer's basic concepts are rooted in a lack of a thorough assessment of his universal outlook, his original and somewhat non-Western ways of thinking. Those misunderstandings of his concepts have happened due to the reluctance of many of his critics to accept his system on the whole and due to their selective reading of his work. But most of all, many of Schopenhauer's concepts are grossly misunderstood, trivialized and rejected due to a lack of appreciation and under-estimation of his Eastern sources. A knowledge of the basics of Indian philosophy may not be essential reading for all students of Western philosophy, but it is so for a serious interpreter of Schopenhauer's thought. Unfortunately, many established Schopenhauer scholars are innocent of Eastern thought and choose to remain, for the most part, silent on the Eastern systems which were deeply and consistently admired, studied and commented upon by this thinker. Although these scholars have done well in pointing out Schopenhauer's connections with the Platonic and Kantian systems, they are either silent or too brief about Schopenhauer's Eastern sources and the impact of Eastern thought on his way of thinking. A comparison of Schopenhauer's basic concepts concerning existence and the world with those of Vedanta and Buddhism, can help to resolve some of the superficial problems and inconsistencies that trouble some interpreters of this thinker's work.

One of the most puzzling things about Schopenhauer for many of his interpreters schooled in Western philosophy is his sharp disdain of the world and existence as such. His rejection of individualism, an all-important Western value, as well as his obsession with suffering and downplaying of happiness makes many of his readers wonder whether this thinker is an extremist. Thus many scholars of Schopenhauer's work have called him an extreme pessimist and have charged him with absurdity, perversity and hypocrisy. Perhaps no other philosopher's life has been so consistently scrutinized to find faults and character flaws as that of Schopenhauer. However, it is quite fair to call him a pessimistic thinker. He clearly rejects optimistic presuppositions such as Leibniz's notion of this world being the best of all possible worlds, and habitually downplays satisfactions and glories of human existence. However, the current secondary literature on Schopenhauer, for the most part, goes too far in turning his pessimism into perversity and eccentricity. His biographers have left no stone unturned in caricaturizing his life-style of a morbid recluse, misanthrope and misogynist and seem to condemn him for not living up to the standards of a purely ascetic life as upheld within his own philosophy.

Among the various concepts of Schopenhauer that are misunderstood in the secondary literature, the ones that stand out are those of the world, existence, asceticism and denial, eternal justice, salvation, and individual existence and its moral possibilities. Schopenhauer's statements such as the following have caused much bewilderment: 'Every individuality is really a special error, a false step, something that it would be better should not be, in fact, something from which it is the real purpose of life to bring us back' (W-II, 492). This is the kind of pronouncement that really puzzles many of Schopenhauer's interpreters, and makes them see superficial problems and inconsistencies in his thought. For example Michael Fox writes:

> The doctrine of *palingenesis* as permulgated by Schopenhauer is indeed difficult to comprehend, and there is more than one lacuna in his account . . . After all, Schopenhauer makes the perverse claim that for mankind it would have been better not to have come into being than to exist; life is merely a disturbing interruption of the blissful non-existence. Schopenhauer's doctrine of self-renunciation must be examined independently of his entirely perverse and absurd position . . . that man is guilty and inexpugnably sinful, not because of his deeds but merely because he exists.[1]

In a similar unsympathetic reaction to Schopenhauer's seemingly pessimistic but philosophically profound statement 'we are at bottom something that ought not to be' (W-II, 507), David Cartwright expresses his displeasure as follows.

> We suffer and die because we deserve it. The world is perfectly retributive. We deserve what we receive because we are guilty. We are guilty because we exist. Schopenhauer's logic is now as clear as it is unconvincing . . . If we explore these claims they seem highly implausible.[2]

The above-mentioned statements of Schopenhauer have received somewhat exaggerated and distorted interpretations by Fox and Cartwright not to mention their frequent use of the negative terms like 'perverse', 'absurd', 'lacuna', 'unconvincing logic', 'implausible', etc. In such statements concerning the nature of the world, of course, Schopenhauer is being very pessimistic. But at the same time he is interpreting classical Vedic and Buddhist beliefs that being born into and thoughtlessly clinging to *samsara* (world or excessive worldliness) is not desirable and hence no event for celebration. This ancient wisdom warns of the dangers of a thoughtless submerging of oneself into excessive and obsessive worldliness. This wisdom also brings the same message through the myth of reincarnation and the law of karma, and especially in Buddhism, in the law of dependent origination. Schopenhauer gave his seal of approval to this Eastern wisdom for he found these critiques of excessive worldliness quite compatible with his own descriptions of the human subservience to the will-to-live. He also finds the laws of karma and dependent origination quite logical and in harmony with the thrust of his own metaphysical system. Although he read all this in his pessimistic way, he found a revalidation of his ideas in these classical sources. This is not to say that Schopenhauer borrowed the fundamentals of his own system, fully promulgated in the first edition of *WWR*, from Eastern philosophy. As he himself mentions, he was pleased to discover the parity of his thought with Eastern systems only subsequently. It was this discovery that made him delve more and more into Vedanta and Buddhism for the rest of his life. Thus, a comparative analysis of Schopenhauer's works with Indian philosophies is not only important but vital for a fuller appreciation of his way of thinking. The absence of such analysis has made him look not only more pessimistic than he is but also to the eyes of some scholars, 'perverse, absurd and illogical'. It has also led some of his biographers to exaggerate his oddities, his gloominess and his offbeat conduct. For instance Bryan Magee writes in the biographical note appended to his *The Philosophy of Schopenhauer*:

> In the light of the present day knowledge there can be little doubt that Schopenhauer's despairing view of the world, above all his conviction of the terribleness of existence as such, were in some degree neurotic manifestations which had roots in his relationship with his mother . . . If actions speak louder than words, his life as in fact he lives it . . . tells us of a man in whom protean pleasures are being experienced side by side with mountainous frustration, misanthropy and desolate miseries of neurosis.[3]

While it is true that Schopenhauer did not have good relations with his mother and was not the one to suffer the company of philistines, it is really an extreme judgement to call him a neurotic. There is evidence that he tried to live according to his philosophy as well as according to his preferences. He chose to live alone, remained unmarried like many other Western philosophers, and devoted himself continuously to his work. He was neither a saint nor claimed to be one. His philosophy upholds the denial of the will and asceticism. In his own way he was an ascetic but not a perfect one. As he himself said, a maker of a handsome sculpture does not have to be handsome himself.

There is no evidence that he enjoyed 'protean pleasures' as alleged by Magee. Perhaps Magee is referring to his large appetite and orders of extra sauces during his lunches at the *Englischer Hof*, mentioned by several biographers. It is common enough for older persons living by themselves to have large appetites. But enough of these cross-references to Schopenhauer's life. Let us return to the philosophical work of the Sage of Frankfurt.

In Buddhism, the bliss of *nirvana* (salvation) is contrasted with the unsatisfactoriness or *dukkha* (suffering) of *samsara* (world). The notion of *nirvana* as a release from the cycle of rebirth is a mythological version of the philosophical insight that *samsara* (or frivolous clinging to the will-to-live) ought not be valued. A life of *dharma* (moral law) must overcome excessive love of the world. According to Vedanta, individuality or ego (*aham*) and self-love (*mamta* or mineness) are the traps for the worldly individual that take him or her further away from the real self (*atman*). Schopenhauer's statement that at bottom 'every individuality is a false step, something that it would be better not be' makes sense in comparison to the Vedantic insight that self-love prevents real knowledge of the self and the Buddhist teaching that in fact there is no self or ego; it is all a chimera. 'Something that it would be better not be' indicates that there are no grounds to value existence absolutely. Coming into being, mere living and love of living is not what is valuable or a cause for celebration. It is ego-less living and being ready to die that depicts a higher life. Schopenhauer's enigmatic pronouncements produce a suffusion of the Western philosophy of death elucidated by Socrates, Plato, Plotinus and other classical Greek and Roman thinkers with Indian thought. In Indian thought the disdain of *samsara, aham* (ego) and *maya* (illusory worldliness) are expressed philosophically as well as in the religious myths of reincarnation, rebirth, karma and nirvana. Thus, Schopenhauer shows his acumen as a universal thinker. Consistent with these Eastern philosophies is Schopenhauer's teaching that the real purpose of human life is to bring ourselves back from the individuality-based, narrow minded existence of the seemingly rational pursuits of the irrational and blind will-to-live. The will-to-live deludes us by making our so-called rational mind a partner in the crimes of the heart.

Many scholars including those from India are critical of Schopenhauer's interpretations of Vedanta and Buddhism and his use and abuse of Eastern concepts within his own system. It is clear that he was a pioneer of trans-cultural philosophy, and his admiration for Eastern thought was remarkable for his day and age. His universal outlook and his treatment of the world's philosophies as a single body of knowledge was something that places him far ahead of his times. However, despite his rigorous study of the materials of Eastern thought available in his time, he may have interpreted Vedanta and Buddhism within the range of his own presuppositions and might not have done justice to some of the other relevant doctrines and concepts of these systems. One of the major critiques of Schopenhauer's interpretation of Eastern thought is regarding the issue of pessimism. It would be unfair to regard either Vedanta or Buddhism pessimistic on the whole and Schopenhauer's attempts to seek the revalidation of his own system in classical Eastern thought may have conveyed that negative impression. Just because these Eastern philosophies are other-worldly in their outlook does not mean that they are pessimistic about this world of here and now.

It is important to keep in mind the history of Schopenhauer's involvement with Eastern thought, even though he claims that the first publication of *WWR* in 1819 was hardly affected by his studies of Indian sources. However, his *Manuscript Remains* that contain his intellectual diary indicate that he had started to read Eastern texts as early as 1813. After the appearance of *WWR*, Schopenhauer was surprised to find the affinity of his metaphysical system with Indian philosophy. It was at this point that he began serious studies of the translations and commentaries of Indian texts, although unlike some other Indologists of the day he did not learn the Sanskrit language systematically. The study of Vedanta and Buddhism, his admired systems of thought, had become a life long scholarly and personal involvement for him. The remainder of his personal library available in the Schopenhauer Archives in Frankfurt contains numerous works on Indian philosophy, including his personal copy of Anquetil Duperron's Latin translation of the Upanishads, a book he adored more than any other. The evidence of his Eastern studies appeared in the form of some additional references to Vedanta and Buddhism in the subsequent editions of *WWR* and numerous citations and comments regarding Indian philosophies in his later works, most notably in the *Will in Nature* and *Parerga and Paralipomena*. All in all, Schopenhauer made a substantive contribution to the popularization and scholarly recognition of Eastern thought in the West.

SCHOPENHAUER AND VEDANTA

The term Vedanta literally means 'the end of the Veda'. The Vedas are the basic scriptures of the Hindus believed to be the oldest books of the world, some parts as old as 5,000 years, containing in them the reservoirs of Indian civilization, orthodox religion, philosophy and culture. The Upanishads are the texts containing philosophical dialogues appended to the Vedas in later centuries. There are four Vedas and more than a hundred Upanishads but only 13 of them are regarded as classical, primarily because these are the oldest. The eighth-century Hindu philosopher Sankara wrote commentaries on 13 Upanishads and believed that these contained the essence of Vedic insight. Thus Vedanta is supposed to be the end of the Vedas in the sense of the Vedic knowledge culminating in the Upanishads, and also the end in the sense of the aim or the essence of the Vedas. Vedanta is a term applied to the central philosophy associated with Hinduism, but it is also the name of one of the six classical philosophical systems of Hindu thought. The advaita (non-dualistic) Vedanta school, of which Sankara was the chief exponent, is one of the sub-systems of the Vedanta system of Hindu philosophy. In sum, Vedanta is a term used for the central and most recognized philosophy of Hindu thought, in itself, offering the essence of the Vedic world-view.

There are three recognized classical texts of Vedanta or Hindu thought in general, namely, the Vedas, the Upanishads and the Bhagvadgita. *Bhagvadgita* or 'The Song of the Blessed One', which itself is a chapter from the Hindu Epic, *Mahabharata*, was elevated to the rank of *Sruti* (revealed knowledge) along with Vedas and Upanishads by all classical exponents of Hindu thought, including Sankara. Whereas the contents of the Vedas and Upanishads are quite unsystematic and full of ambiguities, the *Bhagvadgita*, in contrast, is a lucid and succinct expression of the Hindu world-view, a world classic of religion and philosophy. In addition, there is a body of classical commentarial literature including that of Badryana and Sankara that interpreted the *Sruti* texts into holistic world-views. Schopenhauer was very fond of the Upanishads and the *Bhagvadgita* and quoted from them in his writings consistently. He also read most of the translations and commentaries on Indian thought available in Europe in his times. It is obvious from his writings that Schopenhauer greatly admired the Vedanta school of philosophy. However, his perceptive and creative expositions of Vedanta are not always justified and comprehensive enough. His own validations of atheism, extreme asceticism and pessimism are not in accord with the spirit of Vedanta. His concept of the will-to-live, despite its all-pervasive character, is not comparable to that of *Brahman*, which as the ground of the world is described as *sat-chitta-ananda* (Being-consciousness-bliss) by the Hindu philosopher Sankara. Vedantic thought which became more theistic with the advent of the *Bhagvadgita* is opposed to atheism and pessimism. In book 4 of the *WWR*, Schopenhauer cites the examples of Hindu sadhus, yogis and munis (monks), along with the Christian saints and mystics as the practitioners of the denial of the will-to-live. Although such ascetics and holy men are common in the Hindu tradition, extreme asceticism as such is not recommended by its scriptures. The pursuit of a higher moral life (*dharma*) is not described as a matter of affirmation and denial of the world. In the *Bhagvadgita*, a fusion or union (*yoga*) of action (*karma*), devotion (*bhakti*) and knowledge (*jnana*) is described as vital for an authentic life. Thus action has to be devoted and selfless and designed in the light of the knowledge of *Brahman*, having all these three ingredients at the same time. *Bhakti* is offered as an alternative to asceticism, a method of voluntary love rather than a deliberate stifling of one's desires. Thus Schopenhauer has a good reason to admire Hindu saints, sadhus and yogis, but he seems to oversimplify things by his reading of Hindu doctrines as a combination of asceticism and pessimism.

The concept of will-to-live is often compared with the Vedantic concept of *maya* (illusion, illusory worldliness). Schopenhauer himself considered maya or veil of *maya* as equivalent to his notion of *principium individuationis* as akin to the will-to-live. All in all, Schopenhauer found Vedanta and Buddhism quite conducive to his own approach to reality. While he built his system around the all-pervasive, blind and ultimately meaningless will-to-live, he offered an original critique of the European tradition of rational, representational and calculative thinking as well as a critique of the basic Judeo-Christian presuppositions such as the personal god, man as the unique entity made in the image of god and human being as the measure of all things. He also opposed the historical approach in philosophy. Thus he did not just have a personal contempt for Hegel but opposed all aspects of Hegelianism as the embodiment of all the above-mentioned presuppositions. Through the discovery of the will-to-live he sought to correct the firmly embedded Western notions of a personal god, the supremacy of the rational and the dismissal of the instinct. While Indian concepts did cast a spell on Schopenhauer's thinking, he did not just borrow them to design his notion of the will. He just found these concepts surprisingly akin to his already developed metaphysical system, and in a way able to elucidate the inner nature of the will. He was also able to validate the truth of his own ideas by finding their parallel in the ancient world-views of the Indian civilization.

SCHOPENHAUER AND BUDDHISM

We may surmise that Schopenhauer was impressed with the notion of *dukkha*, the literal meaning of which is suffering or pain. In the very first sermon that the Buddha is supposed to have delivered soon after the attainment of enlightenment (*bodhi*), the term *dukkha* is mentioned several times. This remarkable statement on the nature of human existence in words that produce for many the echo of truth:

> Now this, O monks, is the noble truth of dukkha; the birth is dukkha, old age is dukkha, sickness is dukkha, death is dukkha; sorrow, lamentation, dejection and despair are dukkha. Contact with unpleasant things is dukkha; not getting what one wishes is dukkha. In short, five clusters (*skandhas*) of grasping are dukkha.[4]

It is easy to imagine the impact of this unalloyed statement of human reality on Schopenhauer. Taken in the literal sense all-pervasiveness of dukkha or pain creates the impression that the Buddha has painted a dark picture of life or, a rather pessimistic characterization of human sojourn on this earth. This selective reading of only the first part of the four noble truths may lead to the conclusion that Buddhism emphasizes a pessimistic account of reality. But when we read the noble truths in their entirety, that is, all four of them, we notice that whereas a malady is identified and a bitter truth is unveiled, its cause and its remedy are also offered. Furthermore, if we re-read the first noble truth, keeping in mind what exactly it says and what it does not say, we are led to a more moderate interpretation of the text. What is said is that there are inevitable occasions of dukkha in any life, such as old age and death, some dejections and despairs, having to deal with unpleasant things and non-fulfilment of many a wish. What the first truth does not say is that the entire life is dukkha, or life is nothing but dukkha. It was easy for the Buddha to say: listen O, monks, life (*jivan*) is dukkha. But instead he chose to specify some unavoidable occasions of dukkha, proposing that one must be wise enough to recognize them and strong enough to cope with them. Some sort of pre-preparation and an appropriate moral programme is needed to recognize, accept and properly respond to dukkha that is around the corner. Thus, the Buddha's account of life points towards some specifics; it is not a general statement.

The next three truths are full of optimism of a spiritual kind. The second noble truth identifies the cause of all dukkha, and the third, expresses the faith that *dukkha* can be eliminated 'without a remainder', whereas the fourth and final truth outline the path that leads to the removal of *dukkha*. But before we examine these later portions of the Buddha's first sermon, we must explain what the Buddha means by his opening statement 'the birth (*janma*) is dukkha.' Obviously, Schopenhauer was overwhelmed with this statement for it serves as a foundational stone of his pessimistic view of the world. By being born, one is already doomed. It is hard to find a spark of optimism in this pronouncement on human life. But let us pause. There is more here than meets the eye. While the Buddha offers an original world-view distinct from that of Vedanta, he refrains from being too original. He had to take into account the age-old beliefs of the people he was addressing. Thus he retains the law of karma and the myth of reincarnation which was already existed in orthodox Hinduism. It is also quite fair to assume that he found the law of karma and the possibility of 'rebirth', a modified reincarnation, quite logical and consistent with his own theory of dependent co-origination of all things. Thus, he declares to the monks 'the birth is dukkha,' that is, being born in the world (*samsara*) as such is no cause for celebration. Being caught up in cycle of rebirth and inevitable occasions of *dukkha* is far less preferable to being free and being in *nirvana*. The downplaying of *samsara*, and being free from the trappings of worldly projects, cravings, indulgences and from the false promises of the world is the prerequisite of wisdom. Thus a disease should not be masked with the false claims of health. Being born cannot be called a happy occurrence, because to say so would mean that the world, that is, the *samsara* or the world with the love of worldliness, cannot be called preferable to moral freedom (life of *dharma*) and *nirvana*. Life itself or living in any which way cannot be called preferable to a higher moral life. Therefore the Buddha begins the discourse by realistically acknowledging the fact that being born is already a challenge not to be lost in the singing of the glories of life at the outset. Schopenhauer gladly embraces the literal meaning of the pronouncement of the Buddha in the sense that life is doomed at the outset. He also likes the Buddhist version of reincarnation, that is, rebirth unrelated to any notion of the transmigration of the soul and calls it *palingenesis*. While he finds the Hindu reincarnation based on the theory of the permanence of the soul, which he calls *metampsychosis*, interesting and logical, he prefers the Buddhist *palingenesis*, since it is closer to his own version of the will perpetuating itself through the species, and the individuality facing total annihilation in death.

Thus it would be simplistic to say that the four noble truths which enunciate the essentials of Buddhism, offer a pessimistic account of reality and of human life. However, Schopenhauer fails to highlight the hopeful and morally uplifting tenor of these truths in the way he describes them:

> In [Buddhism] all improvement, conversion and salvation to be hoped from this world of suffering, from this *samsara* proceed from the knowledge of the four fundamental truths: (1) *dolor* (suffering) (2) *doloris ortus* (origin of suffering) (3) *dolaris interitus* (cessation of suffering) (4) *octoparita via ad doloris sedationem* (the eightfold path to the calming of suffering). [W-II, 623]

Schopenhauer reduces the entire detail of the first noble truth to one word, namely, *dolor* or suffering, and interprets *samsara* as the world of suffering. He does acknowledge in his philosophy that human life is the only form of life in which the will has the possibility to deny itself. He views this as possibility to attain real conversion and salvation from this world of suffering, as the only hopeful sign in the four truths. The word *dukkha* is taken in the literal sense of 'suffering' by him, and its larger meaning of unsatisfactoriness of existence or the challenging nature of life is not explored by him.

In the second noble truth, *trishna* (a thirst, craving) is identified as the cause of dukkha; 'Now, this, O monks is the noble truth of the cause of *dukkha*; that craving (*trishna*) which leads to rebirth, combined with pleasure and lust, finding pleasure here and there, namely, the craving for passion, the craving for existence, the craving for nonexistence.' It is also implied that *trishna* that leads to rebirth combines *mythos* and *logos*. This craving is usually a craving for passions (of the world) and a craving for the 'continuation of existence'. At times, it becomes a craving for religious salvation, or nirvana, which is equally doomed because the pursuit of nirvana should not be a craving, but must begin with a giving up of the self. This is the message in the following stanza of the *Visuddhi-magga* scripture: 'Nirvana is but not the man who seeks it, the path exists but not the traveller on it.'[5] That is, giving up of the self and all its cravings is the prerequisite for walking on the road to nirvana. The description of trishna in the second noble truth is so similar to Schopenhauer's account of the will-to-live, which seeks pleasure here and there. The word will-to-live is called a 'pleonasm' by Schopenhauer; it is primarily a will for continued living, a 'craving for existence' as the second noble truth mentions. It is easy to see why Schopenhauer will find a revalidation of his concept of the will-to-live in Buddhist scriptures. However, he fails to get the message regarding the craving for non-existence in the second truth. For his notion of the denial of the will-to-live resembles the craving for non-existence. The Buddha has forewarned that mitigation of the cravings, must not become yet another craving and take the form of extreme asceticism and/or a denial of the genuine needs of the body. Schopenhauer's reduction of the living of an ideal life to a practice of denials may be useful as a guideline but is both artificial and extreme as a way of life.

The third noble truth is the most hopeful and optimistic statement regarding the nature of things:

> Now this O monks, is the noble truth of the cessation of dukkha; the cessation without a remainder of that craving, abandonment, forsaking, release, non-attachment.[6]

This declaration assures us that craving 'without a remainder' is a very much achievable, uncommon but possible prospect for a human life. To achieve detachment and a release from cravings is not a fantastic undertaking but quite realistic for those who resolve to abandon and forsake the bondage to *samsara*. For Schopenhauer, abandonment and forsaking of the machinations of the will or subservience of the will happens alongside the arising of the self-knowledge of the will. Such self-analysis and self-criticism of the will can happen only in human existence for which saying 'nay' to the will's passions is a realistic possibility. Schopenhauer discusses the exemplary lives of ascetics, saints, mystics, sadhus, munis (silent saints) from the Christian, Hindu and Buddhist tradition in book IV of the *WWR*. While he dismisses the religious dogmas of these pious individuals as superstition, he studies their life-styles as examples of the voluntary practice of the denial of the will-to-live. Once again the issue of such detachment from the material world is not discussed as part and parcel of a multi-pronged programme of a spiritual life, or of a life of *dharma* with practice of an all-encompassing thoughtful life as is done in Buddhism.

The fourth noble truths offer such a comprehensive moral programme replete with the practice of compassion and wisdom in all departments of human life.

> This, O monks, the noble truth of the way that leads to the cessation of *dukkha*; this is the noble eightfold path, namely, right views, right intention, right speech, right action, right livelihood, right effort, right mindfulness, right concentration.[7]

This truth brings home the insight that higher life of freedom and nirvana cannot be achieved by doing a single thing. There is no magic formula. By practicing a moderate and well-balanced conduct in all aspects of living in one's views, intentions, speech, actions, livelihood, spiritual efforts, knowledge and meditation, the march towards nirvana begins. The word translated as 'right' in fact is *samma* which means appropriate, well-balanced and moderate. Schopenhauer seems to miss this element of moderation and balance. He hardly paid any attention to the Buddha's prologue to the four noble truths:

> These two extremes, O monks, are not to be practiced by one who has forsaken *samsara*. What are the two? That conjoined with passion . . . and that conjoined with self torture. Avoiding these two extremes the *Tathagata* (Thus-arrived one; the Buddha) has gained the knowledge of the middle way.[8]

Thus according to the Buddha, the thoughtless and vulgar pursuits of passion in the *samsara* driven life, as well as self-torture and needless asceticism are to be avoided. The middle-way in thought and in living is the way to go. Thus Schopenhauer's pessimism and his adoration of asceticism are not in accord with the middle-way recommended by Buddhism.

EPILOGUE

All in all, Schopenhauer's achievement should not be measured by the correctness or incorrectness of his interpretations of Vedanta and Buddhism. It is to be assessed by the substantive contribution he made to the introduction of Eastern thought in the West. The attitude of openness towards philosophies of other cultures, and the treatment of world philosophy as one body of knowledge, is nothing short of devising a new method of philosophizing. His practical example of the use of concepts from different traditions within the elucidation of his own system indicates that in his intellectual horizons, he was able to rise above the boundaries of East and West and many rigid assumptions of his own tradition.

CHAPTER EIGHT

ETHICS AND ETERNAL JUSTICE

It is quite common to divide philosophy into the theoretical and the practical or pure and applied. To do such a thing would be both naïve and artificial according to Schopenhauer. He maintains that all philosophy is always theoretical; it must always have a contemplative attitude and must focus on inquiring rather than prescribing. In other words philosophy does not just define what is good but also explains why the good is good. While Schopenhauer agrees with the previous Western thinkers including Kant that ethical action and the nature of virtue are deeply philosophical issues, he takes the field of ethics a step further. Without letting ethics be a prescriptive knowledge, he includes in it the issues of the desirability or undesirability of existence itself, of the acceptance and rejection of worldly life, of ultimate freedom and salvation. 'For here, where it is a question of the worth or worthlessness of existence, of salvation and damnation, not the dead concepts of philosophy decided the matter, but the innermost nature of man himself' (W-I, 271).

Ethics is a matter of living a life of compassion by gaining a conviction based on an inquiry into the 'innermost nature of man' rather than searching for rational imperatives and maxims applicable to one and all, as conceived by Kant. It is the inquiry into the fundamental status of man and his or her will that reveals to us that empathy rather than rationality is the pathway to true virtue. Virtue must deal with will directly rather than its subordinate functionary, the intellect. Moral systems of philosophy are there to explain rather than moralize or train the deviants: 'Virtue is as little taught as is genius . . . We should therefore be just as foolish to expect our moral systems and ethics would create virtuous noble and holy men, as that our aesthetics would produce poets, painters and musicians' (W-I, 271). Virtue is always a matter of the heart rather than of the intellect. That is why all religions promise reward for the qualities of the heart in the hereafter, and not for the qualities of the intellect, Schopenhauer reminds us. It is empathy (*Mitleid*; literally: suffering-with), not rationality that is the soul of ethics. Here Schopenhauer agrees with the Buddha that the main thing to be reckoned with in existence is suffering (*dukkha*), and proper response to *dukkha* is compassion (*karuna*; literally: melting of the heart).

FREEDOM AND NECESSITY

The will, of which man is the 'most complete phenomenon', is free because it is the thing-in-itself according to Schopenhauer. The phenomenon, however, is always governed by the principle of sufficient reason, that is, has necessity based in it due to the presence of consequents and their grounds. All that is object for the subject is from one point of view ground or reason, and from another a consequent. But the will itself is not subordinate to the principle of sufficient reason. Thus it is never consequent of a reason, nor led by any necessity. It is absolutely free. Freedom therefore is a negative concept, that is, absence or denial of necessity. Whereas man is the most complete phenomenon of the will, he is not an ordinary phenomenon like the objects of the world. Whereas he partakes of the freedom of the will, he also has some necessity, owing to the possession of a distinctive character built into him. Man is a case of the union of freedom with necessity. 'Just as everything in nature has its forces and qualities that definitely react to a definite impression, and constitute its character, so man also has his character, from which motives call forth his actions with necessity' (W-I, 287).

In what sense the freedom inherent in will extends to man in order to make him a special phenomenon, that Schopenhauer calls the most complete phenomenon of the will. First, man is endowed with such a high degree of knowledge that he can fathom the inner nature of the world as a representation. That is, man can apprehend ideas that can be called the 'pure mirror of the world'. In man, will can attain its full self-consciousness and can have knowledge of its own inner nature. Art happens due to the activity of this kind of knowledge of the Ideas, as shown in Schopenhauer's reflections on art and the art forms (see Chapter Five). Man has freedom of a fundamental kind, which never appears in another phenomenon of nature. Will can attain to the freedom of self-denial in man. Will can abolish its own self-nature and yet allow the phenomenon to continue in time to complete its term in existence. In order words, as a result of the highest knowledge of the will's nature prevailing in himself, man can decide to deny or nullify that will, and can possibly live a transformed life of the denial of the will. This is never a complete or absolute transformation. It has to be earned anew in conduct all the time. But such a denial as such, such a freedom from the usual worldliness is a distinctive possibility of man, according to Schopenhauer. Heidegger offers a similar account of authenticity (*Eigentlichkeit*) or attaining of one's own-ness in his analytic of Dasein, which is also not meant to be an absolute or irreversible transformation. Schopenhauer says that in this sense not only the will, but also man can be called free. In this sense, man partakes of the freedom inherent in the will and detaches himself from the necessity of worldliness, while still being in the world.

CHARACTER: INTELLIGIBLE, EMPIRICAL, ACQUIRED

Man is a complete and distinctive phenomenon of the will that is free, should not be taken to mean that an individual human being is not subject to any necessity. It also does not mean that the force of the motives within man is less effective than that of the causes within the objective world. Schopenhauer explains that although an individual is a phenomenon of a free will, he is, in fact, 'the already determined phenomenon' of a free will's free willing. That is, he is a by-product of the free will and thus determined in a sense. As he enters in the form of all objects, that is, the principle of sufficient reason, the unity of that will is split into the plurality of actions. This plurality of his actions appears in subordination of the principle of sufficient reason in the form of the law of motivation, whereas the unity of the free will remains outside time. Thus a human individual is and knows himself or herself as a priori free. However, from a reflection on one's experience, one recognizes oneself to a posteriori subject to a necessity. One learns that one's motives are consistent with a pattern of behaviour or a distinct character.

Schopenhauer points out that Kant was the first to explain the coexistence of a necessity with the freedom of the will in terms of the intelligible and empirical characters of man, and this was Kant's outstanding achievement. Schopenhauer borrows these concepts of

Kant to explain in his own way, how freedom and necessity prevail within all human actions, and to explain why each individual seems to have a changeless character and a distinct personality, never to be duplicated within any other human being.

> The intelligible character of every man is to be regarded as an act of will outside time, and thus indivisible and unalterable. The phenomenon of this act of will, developed and drawn out in time, space and all the forms of the principle of sufficient reason, is the 'empirical character' as it exhibits itself for experience in the man's whole manner of action and course of life. (W-I, 289)

Man was earlier described as the complete phenomenon of the will; complete in the sense of being not only determined by the will but also participating in the freedom of the will. Schopenhauer calls the distinctive intelligible character of an individual an act of will which is time-less. Just as in the objective world, there are numerous Platonic Ideas which are timeless, on the subjective side of reality, there are numerous timeless intelligible characters. Just as an Idea manifests itself in many objects, an intelligible character manifests itself in many acts of the individual which collectively depict his empirical character. While the intelligible character grants a distinctive slant to an individual's actions and interpretations, it is never really known, except through the individual's empirical character, visible in the patterns of his behaviour which is geared by the principle of sufficient reason, in the forms of space, time and the laws of motivation. Our intelligible character gives us the intimations of its existence, but is mostly hidden from us. Thus one never knows who one is, and one never fully knows the why of one's own actions. According to Schopenhauer, all of an individual's needs are the repetitious manifestations of his intelligible character. His empirical character is an 'induction' of the sum of all his actions, judged in an a-posteriori fashion. In other words, the intelligible character is the not fully known origin and source of the action, the empirical character is the better known way in which the actions have already occurred.

Schopenhauer cautions that people often entertain the 'delusion' that they find an absolute freedom of the will in their self-consciousness. He explains that because the will is fundamentally free, the feeling or originality and arbitrariness must appear in self-consciousness along with all its acts, even though all these acts are determined. At the same time, the individual has the illusion of an empirical freedom of his or her will. A feeling of the freedom of the individual acts of consciousness arises due to the way the intellect relates to the will. Schopenhauer explains that in fact, the intellect always knows the decisions of the will a posteriori, that is, after they have happened and their empirical outcome has appeared. Whenever a choice is encountered by the intellect, it has no idea how the will is going to act on it. It is the intelligible character of the person which makes a definite and necessary decision from out of several given motives. But the intelligible character is not known to the intellect. It knows only the empirical character based on the acts of the will after they have already happened. At the same time the intellect has the delusion that two opposite outcomes were equally possible in a given case, having no idea about the already determined decision of the intelligible character. Regarding the choice to be made, the role of the intellect is confined to 'a distinct unfolding of the motives'. It has to await the real decision like a spectator.

There is another reason that the freedom of the will is both misconstrued and misunderstood in the history of Western philosophy, says Schopenhauer. Traditionally, man's inner nature has been described on the basis of the concept of the *soul*, which was conceived to be both a *knowing* and *thinking* entity and only because of its knowing and thinking a *willing* entity. Thus will was given a secondary status and the soul was considered primarily a seat of knowledge (*nous*). Descartes and Spinoza, even called will an act of thought and understood it as judgement. This view led to the belief that man appears in the world as a moral cipher. But Schopenhauer makes no compromises with his firm belief that will is primary and a paramount thing in the Being of man. 'The will is first and original; knowledge is merely added to it as an instrument belonging to the phenomenon of the will' (W-I, 292). Man is born with an original intelligible character. But fundamentally man knows that he is distinct and unlike any other person. 'With those other thinkers, he wills what he knows, with me he knows what he wills' (W-I, 293). Schopenhauer's concept of intelligible character fits very well with his theory of eternal justice, and in a very subtle way is in accord with the law of karma as it appears in Hindu and Buddhist thought. According to this line of thinking, man is not born as a moral clean slate. He has brought the core of his morality and his destiny with him from elsewhere, which will make the slant of his actions seem predetermined, even though the predispositions of his soul are truly self-made. The core of our self is distinct, original and cohesive but for our actions and for our efforts, it is always something yet to be uncovered. The Socratean dictum 'know thyself' assumes a new meaning in Schopenhauer's moral thought.

These allusions to existence of a fixed intelligible character and its mirror image in the empirical character may convey the impression that the individual's own role in shaping his or her destiny is minimal, according to Schopenhauer. Of course the human individual is not merely a passive spectator to the unfolding of his or her intelligible character within an empirical character. To explain the individual's creative role in the building of his character that enables him to make his mark in life, Schopenhauer refers to yet another kind of character, namely, the *acquired character*. The empirical character that an individual encounters appears to have the features of being unalterable and also irrational, like a natural tendency. It would seem that it is needless and pointless to build one's own character or acquire a character in the face of so many unalterable features that are identified as part of one's empirical character. But the reality is different. Although one finds oneself acting, thinking and choosing the same way, one surely does not understand oneself until one has acquired an adequate level of self-knowledge. This self-knowledge obviously comes through experience and reflection.

In trying to know oneself, to recognize one's cherished aspirations, in looking for one's vocation, in learning about one's distinctive abilities that will assure success, a thoughtful person forges ahead in a distinct direction. Schopenhauer remarks that 'our physical path on earth is always a line and not a surface.' In order to possess something worthy we have abandoned many others that fall on the right or the left of the line. A zigzag movement on the surface of life will produce a rolling stone.

> Mere willing and mere ability to do are not enough by themselves, but a man must *know* what he wills, and know what he can do . . . Until he reaches this, he is still without character, in spite of the natural consistency of empirical character. (W-I, 304)

It is only our experience that teaches us the consistent character of our own inner dispositions. It also teaches us that others also possess inflexible characters, which no efforts, no entreaties, no rational arguments can ever alter. We must learn from experience the difference between what we would like to do and what we can do. We must know which ways of life are unsuited to our will that reveals itself in our dispositions. When we have this self-knowledge combined with the worldly knowledge of others, we have obtained our *acquired character*, which is nothing but 'the most complete possible knowledge of our own individuality'. When we have an acquired character, our individuality to us is not just an abstraction or a dogma but is concretely understood in terms of the world and remains the fruit of our own experience. Schopenhauer seems to imply that it is acquired character alone that prepares us to take a heroic attitude against the sufferings of life which are inevitable and which come not in single spies but in battalions. It is hard to imagine anyone who will resolve to live a life of the denial of the will to live, without having developed an acquired character. It is the knowledge of our strong points and our weaknesses that enables us to 'escape in the surest way, as far as our individuality allows, the bitterest of all sufferings (and) dissatisfaction with ourselves' (W-I, 307).

RIGHT AND WRONG AND PUNISHMENT

Egoism is a natural outcome of the affirmation of the will and a matter of course tendency of the human entity. It is only thought or knowledge that enables an individual to overcome the egoism inherent in him, according to Schopenhauer. Under the sway of egoism human being can very easily commit the wrong. Schopenhauer defines wrong and right in terms of his all important notion of the will, or more precisely, in terms of the affirmation of the will. The will produces self-affirmation and love of their own bodies in numerous individuals who happen to be living beside each other in society. Due to egoism inherent in each and every individual, one's affirmation of one's will can easily cross the boundary of another's affirmation of will. An individual may injure or destroy the other's body or compel the other to subserve his own will. 'This breaking through the boundary of another's affirmation of will' is what is denoted by the word wrong (*Unrecht*), according to Schopenhauer. Being an act of the denial of the will of another to promote the affirmation of the will of one, the commission of wrong is never an abstract matter but one that jolts the feelings of both the sufferer and perpetrator; it often

causes physical and mental pain. Schopenhauer cites various, typically wrongful acts like injury, murder, seizure of another's property,
violence and lying in terms of his concept of *wrong* as the conduct
through which one individual 'extends the affirmation of will that
appears in his own body so far that it becomes the denial of the will
that appears in the bodies of other' (W-I, 339).

The concept of right (*Recht*) has its origin in the negation of wrong
or those instances in which wrong by violence was warded off. The
warding off of the violence against oneself or denial of the will in
oneself by another cannot be wrong. Even responding to violence
with violence could be justified by the rightness of one's motives. One
has what Schopenhauer calls a *right of compulsion* to make the perpetrator desist from the denial of one's will. This would also create
a *right to lie* and a right to not cooperate with the inflictor of the
wrong. What Schopenhauer wants to bring home to the reader is that
right and wrong are pure moral determinations that have validity in
an impassioned consideration of human conduct. These concepts
of right and wrong are valid even in the state of nature; these are
not merely conventional notions as the empirically-minded Hobbes
seems to think. The doctrine of right is a chapter of morality, has to
do with *doing* and not with *suffering*, for human actions alone are
manifestations of the will, and its proper subject-matter.

These natural notions of wrong and right are ultimately responsible for the existence of the law and the state, Schopenhauer explains.
We may notice that the German word *Recht* means both *right* and
law. To diminish suffering it was thought reasonable that all men
should renounce 'pleasure to be obtained from doing wrong'. This
explains the origin of the *state contract* or the *law*. In cases of anar-
chy and despotism, the state did not really exist for which a common
accord, and people willing to sacrifice their own good to that of the
society, are required. Schopenhauer maintains that the state exists
'on the correct assumption that pure morality, i.e. right conduct from
moral grounds, is not to be expected. The state, aiming at well-being,
is by no means directed against egoism, but only against the injurious
consequences of egoism' (W-I, 345).

The object of the punishment is 'the fulfilment of the law as a
contract'; but the sole aim of the law is 'to deter from encroachment
on the rights of others'. Thus punishment as the fulfilment of the law
aims at the *future*, and not at the *past*. This aim distinguishes *punishment*

from *revenge,* for revenge is a reaction to what occurred in the past. Retaliation by individuals is not ethically justifiable, nor is evil for evil desirable on any other grounds. The state aims to achieve the safety of society by forbidding all wrongful actions defined as 'criminal' with the threat of punishment, which is actually carried out to make it serve as a real deterrent. Thus, the object of punishment is always to prevent the recurrence of similar criminal acts in the future. To explain this Schopenhauer quotes Seneca's summation of Plato's theory of punishment: 'No sensible person punishes because a wrong has been done, but in order that a wrong may not be done' (W-I, 349).

ETERNAL JUSTICE

The concept of the will necessarily provides for the existence of an *eternal justice* in the world which unlike the *temporary justice* meted out by the state is not dependent on time, nor wavering and imperfect. Schopenhauer maintains that an infallible and in controvertible eternal justice is built into the very nature of things which in many ways is far superior to the temporal justice of human institutions which delivers punishment as a deterrent to secure compliance of the law in future. Schopenhauer seems to imply that whenever we mention a higher tribunal of justice over and above man-made justice, we are not necessarily referring to the kingdom of God, but the very nature of things, the very fact that all existent things are phenomena of the same will, must mean that an eternal justice prevails in the world. We often remark that ultimately things have a way of 'setting themselves aright' or 'in the end truth always prevails' or 'those who do evil deny themselves the good,' etc. In the same spirit Gandhi profoundly says that 'the deniers of God may be many, the deniers of truth there are none.' Whenever we explain these allusions to an invisible tribunal built into the nature of things, we are referring to the eternal justice which Schopenhauer strongly believes existing as part and parcel of the same will that abides in all things.

Schopenhauer's concept of eternal justice has baffled many scholars and interpreters of his thought who are unable to accept his shift from temporal justice, up to which point his thought is crystal clear, towards the higher plane of invisible but infallible eternal justice. They find his speculation hard to accept especially because Schopenhauer sprinkles it with heavy dose of pessimism and a very dark picture of the nature of the world and the destiny of man. Nevertheless, Schopenhauer's belief in the eternal justice is perfectly in accord with classical Greek thinkers such as Heraclitus, Pythagoras and Plato as well as with the law of karma which is an important concept of Hindu and Buddhist thought. It is consistent with the concept of *logos* as well as those of *dharma* and *karma*. The myths of the reincarnation of the souls, prevalent in Hinduism as well as in ancient Greek thought, and a subtle modification of it as rebirth based on cumulative karma in Buddhism, these are all different way of expressing the logical truth that 'the world itself is the tribunal of the world' (W-I, 352). Schopenhauer quotes Euripides to illustrate that actions of men have their immediate reward or punishment, and infallible moral repercussions: 'The whole of heaven would not be great enough to contain the sins of men, were Jove to record them all, nor would he . . . assign to each his punishment. No! The punishment is already here, if only you will see it' (W-I, 351).

However, what Schopenhauer is referring to is neither a myth nor something based on religious dogma. He tries to prove by a philosophical analysis that the omnipresence of the will necessarily entails eternal justice. This bond between all existent things assures an ultimate fair play and due compensation for all deeds done by man or animal. Of course this eternal justice is not visible like the temporal justice delivered by the courts and judges. But it has to be there if all phenomena of the will are inter-connected and are objects of the same thing-in-itself. Thus we can safely conclude that 'all that happens or indeed can happen to the individual, justice is always done to it' (W-I, 351). Accordingly Socrates says with conviction in the *Apology*, 'nothing bad can happen to a good man.' Schopenhauer remarks in his pessimistic interpretation that when we want to consider man's moral worth in general, we cannot ignore that his existence necessarily contains want, suffering, lamentation and certainty of death. Were there no original sin to be expiated or a sentence to be carried out, the human existence would not be as it is, full of suffering and doomed to various hazards and death. The blind will-to-live in man makes him pay little attention to the facts of existence, but prompts him to seek whatever gratifications he can obtain and whatever mastery he can exercise over other phenomena of the world. Little does he appreciate that thing-in-itself is one and the same, but he witnesses only the diverse objects in time and space through the *principium individuationis*; his eyes covered with the *veil of maya* as Hinduism describes the hiddenness of the ultimate unity of all things. In his limited knowledge governed by the principle of sufficient reason, the human subject 'sees not the inner nature of things, which is one, but its phenomena as separated, detached, unnumerable' (W-I, 352). He considers pleasure and pain as two different things, pleasure as desirable and pain as avoidable. The human individual differentiates between the murderer and the victim, between the rich and the poor. According to Schopenhauer, he runs after pleasures and joys of life and does not realize that by his very affirmations of the will, he has embraced sufferings and negative outcomes. The better knowledge of the unity of all eludes him when he does not refrain from exploiting others and denying and intruding upon their will's affirmation to advance his own will. He does not have the vision to know that cumulative suffering of the whole world is his own for he lacks empathy. He confines himself to his actual and possible sufferings as an individual.

But eternal justice is recognized only by one who can see beyond the principle of sufficient reason, to the common origin and common being of all things, the thing-in-itself, which is unified, free and omnipresent. Such a person then 'sees that the difference between the inflictor of suffering and he who must endure it, is only phenomena. . . . The former is mistaken in thinking that he does not share the torment, the latter in thinking that he does not share the guilt' (W-I, 354). Schopenhauer reminds us that the vivid knowledge of the eternal justice will always be out of reach of most people, nor will they readily recognize the related virtue of empathy. They can easily dismiss this line of thinking because it urges them to take a step above the rational and worldly thinking which regards only the range of the principle of sufficient reason as the real sphere of things. Schopenhauer says that the Upanishadic dictum *tat tvam asi* (that thou art) best describes the reality that all things are bound together and emanate from the same unity. Schopenhauer calls it the will, but the Vedanta system calls it *brahman*. Whereas both these notions are of a unifying being of all existents, it would be wrong to treat them as comparable. *Brahman* is called 'ever-existent and blissfully pure consciousness' whereas will, according to Schopenhauer a blind urge to exist, gratify and procreate. Schopenhauer often uses peculiar interpretations of Vedantic and Buddhist concepts to subserve his system.

COMPASSION AS THE SOUL OF ETHICS

We might be led to believe that moralizing that lacks argument, may have some impact on the moral conduct of the individual. According to Schopenhauer, mere moralizing usually fails to motivate. Even what seems to motivate greatly may not have moral worth if it exploits egoism. The genuine virtue does not arise due to rational knowledge either- or by the extensive use of abstractions and arguments, maintains Schopenhauer. Genuine and real virtue is based on an 'intuitive knowledge that recognizes in another's individuality the same inner nature as in one's own' (W-I, 368). Genuine moral excellence or virtue is a matter of disposition and has to do with compassion.

What is this intuitive knowledge that has a direct impact on virtue and why is conceptual knowledge unable to do so? Intuitive knowledge is not the kind that is communicable in words. If it were so, one could teach virtue to another. Schopenhauer points out that virtue can no more be taught than the systems of aesthetics can teach anyone how to be a poet. Just as the concept cannot produce art, it cannot produce virtue. Schopenhauer's insight is valid because we know that a professor of ethics is not necessarily a morally upright person, and instances of unfairness, racism and flawed hiring practices are as rampant in the universities as they are in the general society. By asserting that 'will cannot be taught' (*velle non discitur*), Schopenhauer points towards the difference between willing and conceptualizing which is rooted in the fact that will is free and not bound by conceptual knowledge which uses abstract, discursive concepts of reason. As explained in the section on the world as representation in *WWR*, the immediate representation of perception is only subsequently interpreted by concepts of reason (W-I, 35). Thus neither the abstract dogmas nor the abstract reason directly affects virtue, which classically means 'moral excellence' and Schopenhauer here explains as 'goodness of disposition' (W-I, 368). However, abstract reasoning does perform a function; it enables the individual who is virtuous due to a superior disposition, to comprehend his own moral attitude in terms of concepts, thereby putting together an accountability for his own faculty of reason. In other words, he attempts to interpret and spell out his moral attitude in rational terms for himself, correctly or incorrectly, he shall never know. For fundamentally disposition of the will can never be exactly put into words. We can only approximately judge the actions that are the outcome of the will.

Dogmas and religious teachings seem to have an influence on conduct, and so do customary ways of a people, and examples set up by the leaders and saints. According to Schopenhauer, these influences on the outward actions of people occur because most of them do not trust their own judgement, that is, they find it convenient to be followers of custom and experience of others, being too aware of their own weakness and inability to do an original ethical assessment. The religious dogmas also have a great deal of self-love or egoism built into them and are found to be attractive due to the utter clarity of their moral formulas. In cases of religious dogmas assuming a violent form, Schopenhauer says that one who burns a heretic is no different from a bandit who murders to claim a payment, since these crimes of religion and acts of terror are done to earn a place in heaven, and rooted in egoistic superiority of one's own faith (W-I, 369).

> It would be bad business if the principle thing in a man's life, his *ethical worth that counts for eternity*, depended on something whose attainment was so very much subject to chance as are dogmas, religious teachings, and philosophical arguments. (W-I, 368; italics mine)

The true source of morality in one is not something subject to time and chance. It is something as timeless and free as the will itself, essentially indefinable but inalterably there as part and parcel of one's intelligible character. Not to recognize the moral significance of the world of which man's ethical worth is part and parcel is a wrong philosophical approach; doctrines based on materialism represent the real perversity of mind. As Schopenhauer remarks in *Parerga and Paralipomena*: 'That the world has only a physical and not a moral significance is a fundamental error . . . the real perversity of the mind' (PP-II, 201). The myths of reincarnation say that it is the cumulative karma of many past lives that shapes the current inner disposition, or *svabhava* as it is called in Buddhism, and which is one of the five clusters of grasping (*skandhas*) that constitute a human entity.

Although the true source of morality is eternal and not directly available to the faculty of reason, the individual can have an intuitive knowledge of it through one's own disposition, and through a recognition that in others individualities abides the same inner nature as in one's own. Schopenhauer transforms the Vedantic concept of knowledge (*jnana*) regarding the vision of the *atman* (soul) abiding in all entities, which is expressed in the Upanishads as *tat tvam asi* (that thou art) in his own terminology as 'the will in me is the same as the will in all things.' When one realizes that another's weal and woe is no different from one's own, the pre-existing disposition prompts one towards a moral life and a moral conduct. At the summit of the intuitive ethical knowledge is the will's self-realization, or an individual's realization of the pointlessness and inherent suffering contained in all of his or her actions, prompted by his or her life's saga of the various affirmations of the will. This realization prompts the individual to see through the machinations and traps of the will, to arrive at the conviction that one must lead a life of the denial of the will, an ascetic life, which Schopenhauer finds reflected in the lives of saints and ascetics. Although Schopenhauer does not seem to accept any compromises in his view of asceticism, the realization of the traps of raging and surging will in oneself, can inspire one to lead a simpler, moderate personal life and a life of compassion and loving kindness.

The will can be approximated only in the motives. But motives cannot alter the will itself, they can only change the way will manifests itself. By a study of the actions alone we cannot make a moral judgement of the other's conduct. Schopenhauer maintains that actions are in themselves empty figures. It is the disposition behind the action that gives actions their moral importance. Why does Schopenhauer emphasize the disposition rather than an analysis of human actions that most other philosophical systems are preoccupied with? It is because the dispositions are the basic inclinations of willing, whereas actions are the conceptualized outcomes of that willing. The same disposition can produce a variety of actions, some quite discordant with each other. The same degree of wickedness and egoism can surface as murder and cannibalism in one nation, and as court intrigues, and political manoeuverings, subjugation of the weak through exploitation and war at home and abroad, in another so-called civilized democratic nation. The same disposition can produce very different external realities. Thus a mere superficial analysis of actions and motives does not arrive at the heart of the ethical matter, until it arrives at the disposition to the existence or non-existence of compassion, the ground of which is the sameness of the will in all, in us and in them.

The intuitive knowledge of the ground of virtue cannot be put into words, cannot be reasoned away, but reflects itself in pattern of deeds of a person, in his or her conduct. The person who refrains from denying the affirmation of will in others, even where no state or law interdicting it is watching over it, is truly *just*. Schopenhauer says that the disposition of justice prompts some individuals like Pascal or St Francis of Assisi or some Hindu rajas to embrace voluntary poverty; current examples being Gandhi and Mother Teresa. Whereas a strong distinction imposes itself on most individuals between their own ego and another's is due to the *principium individuationis* that defines separation of phenomena. But for an individual with a truly moral disposition this distinction is not absolute. The suffering of the other seems to him quite like his own suffering. The next step in this empathy is that such an individual denies himself his privileges in a bid to strike a balance between the have and the have-nots, and his having realized the pointlessness of the unbridled affirmation of his own will. Such a moral individual begins to live in all living things, and does not cause pain even to the animal. Schopenhauer was one of the first Western philosophers to recognize and argue for the rights of animals, condemning the cruelty to animals in many of his own writings.

The performance of a disinterested deed gives us a strange satisfaction as we get in touch with our 'good conscience'. According to Schopenhauer, such action without a trace of egoism, verifies that within us exists a knowledge of our kinship with everything that lives. Through such altruistic action, our heart feels enlarged. In fact the inner knowledge of our bond with others, made us feel like doing such a deed. Schopenhauer spells out his original approach to ethics which is unlike other Western philosophers including Kant. Schopenhauer disagrees not only with the rational methods of Kant and his preoccupation with the moral laws and oughts, but also with his reference to human dignity. He pooh-poohs Kant's notion of 'the dignity of man', which fails to find a credible ground of morality. The circular argument of morality resting on dignity, and dignity on morality, does not explain the source of morality within man. Furthermore, Schopenhauer says in his pessimistic tone: 'The notion of dignity could be applied only ironically to a creature like man, who is sinful in will, so limited in intellect . . . so feeble in body' (PP-II, 202). What Schopenhauer implies is that the very being of man, and of every other animal contains within it the entire will-to-live. 'Every individual even the most insignificant, every "I" seen from within is all in all; seen from without he is nothing' (W-II, 600). Being connected and related to all existents cannot be narrowed down to an assumed dignity of man. Although man alone is able to fathom his own will and its universality, to give him a privileged status would be anthropocentricism inconsistent with the fact that nature can destroy man as easily as it can annihilate an insect. Man's actual conduct towards his fellow beings scarcely gives him a badge of dignity or of morality.

Whereas other thinkers have come up with 'precepts for virtue and laws necessarily to be observed', Schopenhauer says that he has 'no *ought* or *law* to hold before the eternally free will'. What concludes his thought on the subject of ethics is as follows: 'All love (*agape*, *caritas*) is compassion or sympathy' (W-I, 374). Schopenhauer remarks in his *On the Basis of Morality* that ancient Greek thinkers, including Plato, failed to include 'loving-kindness' (*agape*, *caritas*) as a cardinal virtue. It was first called a virtue, even the greatest virtue by Christianity. In word and in deed Christianity extolled the love of the neighbour and even called for loving of the enemy. But in Asia 'a thousand years earlier, the boundless love of one's neighbour has been the subject of theory and precept as well as of practice in Veda, dharma-sastras . . . as well as the teaching of the Buddha' (BM, 163). Loving-kindness is called *karuna* (empathy; literally, melting of the heart) in Buddhism and repeatedly advocated in the ancient discourses (*sutras*) of the Buddha.

The influence of Vedanta is unmistakable on Schopenhauer's theories of ethics. Regarding the bond that exists owing to the sameness of the will in all, he remarks: 'I do not know how this truth can be more worthily expressed than the formula: *tat tvam asi* (that thou art).' He acknowledges the debt of his moral philosophy to Vedanta in his final work *Parerga and Paralipomena* as follows: 'The readers of my ethics know that with me the foundation of morality rests ultimately on the truth that has its expression in the Veda and Vedanta . . . *tat tvam asi*, which is stated in reference to every living thing' (PP-II, 219).

CHAPTER NINE

DEATH, PHILOSOPHY AND AFTER-LIFE

The issue of death is the central problem of Schopenhauer's philosophical system. His metaphysics revolves around the single fundamental reality, namely, the will-to-live. Regarding his philosophical enterprise he says that his 'whole work is the unfolding of a single thought' (W-I, 285). This single thought is obviously regarding the will-to-live. The connection between will-to-live and death cannot be denied. The will recoils from death and yet in the case of the human entity, death is always to be reckoned with in the life of the mind. Death has both an explicit and implicit impact on man's way of being. One has an explicitly rational recognition as well as a gut feeling about one's mortality whereby one develops an anxious attitude to cope with this knowledge and feeling. Schopenhauer explores all these nuances of the presence of death in human life, and thus he can be recognized as a philosopher of death (a *thanotologist*) in the Socratean tradition, which regards only contemplators and practitioners of death as true philosophers. It is also to be noticed that the denial of the will-to-live has been exposed as an authentic practice of death by Schopenhauer, as a mark of superior human wisdom. Thus, no other subject is as important and as omnipresent in Schopenhauer's system as death, with the exception of that of will-to-live which is but a constant evasion of death.

DEATH AND PHILOSOPHY

In his celebrated essay on Death in volume 2 of *WWR*, Schopenhauer begins with the remark that the presence of death in human life is the foremost inspiration for the philosophers to philosophize. 'Death is the real inspiring genius or muse of philosophy and for this reason

Socrates defined philosophy as a "practice of death". Indeed without death there would hardly have been any philosophizing' (W-II, 463).

If philosophy arises out of a wonder about the nature of things as Aristotle says, the meaning and implications of death arouse our boundless amazement about the fragile status of human existence. Hence, Socrates named death as the foremost theme of philosophy, and the acceptance and practice of death as the prerequisites of a genuinely philosophical life. Schopenhauer embraces this Socratean dictum regarding the fundamental bond between death and philosophy within his own system. His preoccupation with death shows itself in his all important notion of existence as will-to-live as well as in his portrayal of an ideal human life as a denial of the will-to-live. The denial of the will-to-live is very much comparable to what Socrates calls the practice of death. Furthermore, the fact that Schopenhauer regards death as the muse of his own philosophy is indicated by his various explicit discussions of the meaning and implications of death in many of his early and later philosophical writings. More important is the fact that the issue of death is implicitly present in his major concepts.

According to Schopenhauer, although animals as embodiments of the will-to-live recoil from the danger to their lives just as humans do, they are obviously not aware of their mortal status. The faculty of reason constantly informs man of his certain death. Thus, the reflecting mind always designs some metaphysical interpretations of death in order to cope with the terrible reality of the impending death. All religions and philosophical systems provide such metaphysical resolutions and function as 'antidotes to the certainty of death', although some religions and philosophies do so better than others. Schopenhauer asserts that the doctrines of Hinduism and Buddhism regard arising and passing away as superficial and enable their believers to look death calmly in the face. This is not the case with those faiths which consider man as a creature made out of nothing, namely Judaism, Christianity and Islam (W-II, 463).

Any careful reader of Schopenhauer's body of work cannot fail to notice that in it philosophy and death are shown to be intimately connected. While he has successfully shown that the reality of death is what inspires and sets into motion the activity called philosophizing, and no existential thinking is complete without an analysis of death, he has also attempted to outline the meaning of death along with its existential implications. At the same time, he has not shied away from a comprehensive account of death and its aftermath through a creative combination of religious thought and philosophy. He has also shown that philosophy is not just an abstract speculation about the nature of reality, but it must be relevant to the project of living. Thus, he offers an original analysis of life as it is, along with examples from everyday life, based, of course, on his own presuppositions and the ground-concepts of his system. Death, therefore, as something embedded in life receives his foremost intellectual attention. The acceptance, the welcoming and the practice of death in life are the outstanding human virtues that he seeks to highlight. He regards the outlining of such possibilities of a contemplative life as the chief business of philosophy.

DEATH AND AFTER-LIFE

According to Schopenhauer, the common opinion generally vacillates between the view that death is absolute annihilation and that we are, 'so to speak, with skin and hair, immortal'. Both of these notions are equally false. Death is usually taken as a great misfortune and as a loss, and the mere thought of it arouses dread. It is considered great evil because it signifies absolute annihilation. The fear of death and the negative judgement regarding it could not have come from knowledge, but its source has to be the will-to-live, says Schopenhauer. For knowledge must take into account the evils of life. 'That death is a serious matter could already be inferred from the fact that, as everyone knows, life is no joke' (W-II, 465). The reason for our boundless attachment to life is obviously the will-to-live. This attachment is both irrational and blind and, to the will, life is the highest good. Knowledge opposes attachment to life for it offers both a metaphysical consolation concerning death and discloses life's worthlessness, Schopenhauer asserts in his pessimistic manner. This is why the triumph of knowledge over will is honoured as great and noble in the case of the selfless and the brave men who face death courageously. Those who receive death with despair and strive to cling to life at all costs are deemed as weak and contemptible.

Schopenhauer points out that somehow the issue of our state after death is discussed 'ten thousand times' more than our state before birth. In fact, one is as much of a problem as the other, because there is no reason to believe that non-existence after death has to be different from non-existence before birth. Schopenhauer is preparing the ground for a consideration of the presence of something within us, which always was and always will be.

As classical thinkers like Plato and Epicurus have pointed out, it is absurd to regard death as evil. Schopenhauer remarks that Epicurus was quite right in reminding us that 'when we are, death is not, and when death is, we are not. To have lost what cannot be missed is no evil' (W-II, 468). This again shows that fear of death is not rooted in the intellect but in blind will, whose nature is to crave existence above everything else.

The death of an individual, that is, of a particular phenomenon of the universal force active in numerous similar phenomena, does not imply the cessation of that force itself, just as the stopping of the spinning wheel does not indicate the death of the spinner. This universal life principle, active in all things alive is the will-to-live, which is the indestructible element. Thus, death cannot be regarded as the entire destruction of a human being because the will that propelled it lives on, albeit in other shapes and forms. What transpires in nature reveals that she is indifferent towards life and death of the individual. Nature seems to care much more about the perpetuation of the species. Schopenhauer remarks that

[n]ow since nature abandons without reserve her organisms constructed with such inexpressible skill, not only to predatory instinct of the stronger, but also to the blindest chance, . . . she expresses that the annihilation of these individuals is a matter of indifference to her, does her no harm. . . . With man she does not act otherwise than she does with animals. (W-II, 474)

Schopenhauer maintains that this insight concerning something universal in the particular as the inner being of everything according to Plato's doctrine of Ideas, was vivid in those 'sublime authors of the Upanishads of the Vedas'. Kant's teaching that our intellect does not comprehend the true essence of things but merely phenomena leads to the same path (W-II, 476). Thus, death should be looked at in the light of this fundamental insight of the ancient sages and major philosophers, which leads us to the conviction that 'the true inner being of everything, which, moreover evades our glance everywhere and is thoroughly mysterious, is not affected by that arising and passing away' (W-II, 474). The operations of this invisible being of all things are evident in animal life provided we rise above our supposed superiority over and distinctness from other entities endowed with life. Schopenhauer remarks that the animals of many kinds which come into existence at all times and seem to be full of vitality and drive could never have been nothing before coming into existence.

> Thus everything lingers only for a moment, and hurries on to death. The plant and the insect die at the end of the summer, the animal and man after a few years; death reaps unweariedly. But despite all this, in fact as if this were not the case at all, everything is always there and in its place, just as if everything was imperishable . . . Death is for the species, what sleep is for the individual, or winking for the eye. (W-II, 478, 479)

The will is embedded in and manifests itself, first and foremost in the Idea or the species. Thus, a study of nature reveals that the will is really concerned with the continuance of the species, and it has little regard for the individual. Nature's care for the species over the individual is nature's way of expressing the reality of the Ideas over entities. Nature seems to express the truth that only the Ideas are real, and not the individuals. However, we may question Schopenhauer's excessive reliance on Plato's theory of Ideas by taking into account the fact that, within nature, examples of the extinction of some species can be found. The species are more durable than the entities, but even the species may not be permanent. All living things, animals as well as humans, seem to have a confidence and serenity with which they move about through hazards and chances that could cause their instant death any moment. Schopenhauer believes that this peace and serenity of animals and humans against possible death springs from a deeper consciousness of imperishability that each and every living thing has. This strange confidence that defies the intellectual awareness of possible and certain death, in the case of humans, must be rooted in a deep seated realization that there is no threat to the continuation of the species. The confidence of the species translates itself as the practical and instinctual defiance of death that enables the human beings to be engrossed in their worldly projects. Unlike Heidegger who calls the forgetfulness of death as a project of inauthenticity and one's belonging to the world of the they (*das Man*), Schopenhauer explains this confidence against death as something natural and instinctual. According to him, it has to do with the will's inner realization that it shall always be there through the species, which unlike the individuals, is imperishable. Schopenhauer creatively applies Plato's theory of Ideas to expose that there is something in man's inner being that is untouched by death.

This vital force in us, that is, the will-to-live shows itself in the form of hunger and an instinctual fleeing from death with respect to the individual. However, with respect to the species, the same force gives rise to the sexual impulse and an instinctual desire to have and nurture the offspring. However, all evidence points towards the fact that individuality of the individual that he or she values above everything else is really something unimportant for the will. It seems to use the individual as a means to the higher end of the perpetuation of the species. Schopenhauer suggests that to say enough is enough regarding our own individuality is the sign of highest wisdom. Therefore, the highest ranking thinkers and saints have shown a detachment from self-love and the love of life in their exemplary lives. 'It seems just as absurd to desire the continuance of our individuality, which is replaced by other individuals, as to desire the permanence of the matter of our body, which is constantly replaced by fresh matter' (W-I, 277). We may notice here that Schopenhauer is putting into practice his declaration that 'philosophy is an antidote to the certainty of death'.

DEATH AND THE WORLD

As part of his meditations on the meaning of death, Schopenhauer offers valuable insights on the human entity's connection with its world. These reflections on the man–world relation seem to have influenced subsequent philosophy including that of Nietzsche and Heidegger. Regarding man's interminable bond with the world he says:

> We are far more at one with the world than we usually think. . . . The difference between the continuance of the external world after his death and his own continuance after death will vanish for one who could bring this unity or identity of being to distinct consciousness. . . . The world is no less in us than we are in it, and the source of all reality lies within ourselves. (W-II, 486, 487)

Schopenhauer is here dwelling on the existential as well as the metaphysical implications of the man–world relationship. In fact, from the existential point of view, it is not even a relation because man and world are mutually foundational, and one cannot persist without the other. As Heidegger will put it, man's being is always a being-in-the-world. But unlike Heidegger, Schopenhauer takes it to a metaphysical level. Man realizes his continuation after death in the truth that he continues through all things that are in being at all times. His inner being was always at one with being of everything else. The will in him is the will in everything which continues on despite the lawful passing away of its phenomena. Schopenhauer is certainly taking a cue from his study of the Upanishads and his much admired philosophy of Vedanta, which maintains that all things are pervaded by *Brahman* as the soul (*atman*) of all beings which never perishes but changes its forms (bodies). It also maintains that one's larger self (*atman*) is more important than one's narrower individuality or ego (*aham*); and at a higher level of knowledge (*jnana*) one's own self is viewed as the self (*atman*) of everything that exists.

Schopenhauer rejects the notion that all existents have originated out of nothing as the handiwork of a creator God and will pass into nothing. He rather subscribes to a cyclical notion of the universe and finds the law of karma subscribed by Hinduism and Buddhism quite logical, although he critically examines and modifies its details with respect to the possibility of reincarnation (*metempsychosis*) and re-birth (*palingenesis*) within his own theory of after-life rooted in the concept of the imperishability of the will-to-live. What he finds most satisfactory about Hinduism and Buddhism is the fact that they view the world (*samsara*) as a cycle of birth and death: 'Brahmanism and Buddhism . . . quite consistently with a continued existence after death, have an existence before birth, and (maintain that) the purpose of this life is to atone for the guilt of that previous existence' (W-II, 488). Schopenhauer continues to regard the Christian notion of original sin and the Eastern notion of karma quite logical, when he says 'what exists necessarily exists. Consequently, everyone has to conceive himself as a necessary being. . . . He who conceives his existence as merely accidental, must certainly be afraid of losing it through death' (W-II, 488, 489).

But the urge for salvation must surpass the urge for the continuation forever of one's individuality, which is both undesirable and unlikely in the scheme of things. The love of one's own self and the obsession with one's individuality, which is ultimately superficial and a mere phenomenon of the will, is an error. Schopenhauer goes against the grain of Western preoccupation with individuality and the self in this powerful assertion:

> To desire immortality for the individual is really the same as wanting to perpetuate an error forever; for at bottom, every individuality is a special error, a false step, something that it would be better should not be, in fact something from which it is the real purpose of life to bring us back. (W-II, 492)

What Schopenhauer means by his apparently radical statement that 'every individuality is a special error' should be interpreted in the light of his critique of egoism and the basic assumption of his philosophy that the will abides in everything and individuality is a temporary phenomenon of the will. To cling to the individuality will amount to taking the affirmation of the will too far and shutting the doors to the higher knowledge that prompts human beings to freely deny that will and to lead a truly ethical life. These assertions also indicate Schopenhauer's vote of confidence in the Vedantic and Buddhist beliefs that to repeatedly return to *samsara* (the world-cycle) and to be endlessly subjected to a worldly (will-affirming) life is not a desirable prospect for human destiny. Salvation (*nirvana*) is precisely defined by these systems as the freedom from *samsara*.

DEATH, WILL AND THE ETERNAL IN US

A reflection on the meaning of death reveals the nature of the force that sustains life. Schopenhauer maintains that man as phenomenon is certainly perishable but his inner being is not. This inner being, that is the will-to-live, is named as the same thing as the thing-in-itself, declared as unknowable by Kant. Schopenhauer explains his own position regarding the thing-in-itself as follows:

> We must here keep in mind that we have not, like Kant, absolutely given up the ability to know the thing-in-itself; on the contrary we know that it is to be looked for in the will. It is true that we have never asserted an absolute and exhaustive knowledge of the thing-in-itself. . . . We know our own will always only as a phenomenon,

and not according to what it may be absolutely in and by itself. (W-II, 494)

In the Western philosophical tradition the inner substance of man has been identified as the soul (*psyche*). This soul was primarily understood as the seat of knowledge. Schopenhauer breaks with this tradition by considering something other than knowledge or intellect as the inner being of man. While reflecting on death and after-life, he becomes convinced that the will remains the primary substantiality of man while the intellect, that man alone among all living things is endowed with, is something secondary. Regarding this issue, he clearly writes:

The sharp distinction between will and knowledge, together with the former's primacy, a distinction that constitutes the fundamental characteristic of my philosophy, is therefore the only key to the contradiction . . . that death is our end, and yet we must be eternal. . . . All philosophers have made the mistake of placing that which is metaphysical, indestructible, and eternal in the *intellect*. It lies exclusively in the will, which is entirely different from the intellect, and alone is original. (W-II, 495)

This original insight of Schopenhauer regarding the primacy of the will has influenced subsequent thinkers, most notably Nietzsche and Freud. It also constitutes a fundamental critique of Plato's idealism and the idealistic tradition, even though Schopenhauer expressly follows Platonism with respect to the problems of representation and perception. Based on his notion of the primacy of the will, Schopenhauer explains the connection between consciousness and death. He maintains that 'with death consciousness is certainly lost, but not what produced and maintained consciousness. Life is extinguished, but . . . not the principle of life' (W-II, 496). All human beings have a feeling of having an imperishable element in them, even though they know that death is certain. But they do not know clearly what this imperishable element in them is. It is neither consciousness nor the body, for the consciousness itself is an off-shot of the body. The imperishable and the eternal within man must be something on which both the body and the consciousness depend. 'It is, however, just that which by entering into consciousness, exhibits itself as will' (W-II, 496). Schopenhauer points out that we can only encounter the immediate phenomenal appearance of the will, because we cannot experience it beyond the consciousness. Thus, according to Schopenhauer, what the will might be, other than its appearance in consciousness, or what it might be absolutely in itself, cannot be known. But we can safely conclude that 'the entire will-to-live is in the individual as it is in the race, and thus the continuance of the species is merely the image of the individual's indestructibility' (W-II, 496). What Schopenhauer means to suggest is that one's indestructibility beyond death can only be appreciated by those who overcome their obsession with the individuality, and realize their kinship with the entire kingdom of the will, especially, the being of the entire human race.

The fear of death does not stem from the intellectual knowledge of the certainty of death, but directly from the will, according to Schopenhauer. 'Just as we are allured into life by the wholly illusory inclination for sensual pleasure, so are we firmly retained in life by the fear of death, certainly just as illusory' (W-II, 498). Although the will is assured of its continuation and eternity, its blind thrust is towards life; it is will-to-live. Knowledge teaches us that death is not evil, as many philosophers have demonstrated with convincing argument. The fear of death is rooted in the will, for by nature it recoils from the threat to life. This is why, says Schopenhauer, that all religions and philosophies promise a reward in eternity for the virtues of the heart (i.e. the will) and not for the virtues of the intellect.

We have all often wondered about a contradiction in human nature. On the one hand, all human beings are aware of their certain death and the fact that it is possible any moment. On the other hand, people seldom brood over death and go through life as if death is of no immediate concern to them. Each one of us is able to say to oneself death certainly and lawfully occurs to all human beings, but 'right now it has nothing to do with me,' as Heidegger spells out the typical inauthentic attitude towards death. In the Hindu epic *Mahabharata*, the oldest of Pandava brothers, Yudhishtra, calls this contradiction within humans the wonder of all wonders. Schopenhauer attributes this serenity against death to the self-assurance that the will within us has regarding its own survival against all odds. He outlines and explains this human enigma as follows:

> Man alone carries about with him in abstract concepts the certainty of his own death, yet this can frighten him only very rarely and at particular moments, when some occasion calls it up to

the imagination. Against the mighty voice of nature, reflection can do little. In man, as in the animal that does not think, there prevails as a lasting state of mind the certainty, springing from innermost consciousness, that he is nature, the world itself. By virtue of this, no one is noticeably disturbed by the thought of certain and never-distant death. (W-I, 281)

DEATH AND THE WORLD

Schopenhauer indicates that the fear of death stems from the artificial separation between the individual and the world, produced by the *principium individuationis*. In fact, the individual and the world are co-foundational; one does not make sense without the other. It shows us that Schopenhauer was convinced of the Being-in-the-world of man, which Heidegger treats at length in his *Being and Time*. Schopenhauer exposes the inseparation of man and world in very simple words invoking his all important notion of the will: 'This world will accompany the will as inseparably as a body is accompanied by its shadow; and if will exists, then life, the world, will exist' (W-I, 275). However, unlike Heidegger, Schopenhauer emphasizes the metaphysical and spiritual meanings of Being-in-the-world which inform us about man's destiny beyond death, whereas Heidegger's musings remain strictly existential or this-worldly. Schopenhauer continues to treat individuality as a grand illusion, in the manner of Vedanta philosophy. Although unlike Vedanta, which regards the ultimate reality (Brahman) as everlasting bliss and pure consciousness, Schopenhauer's absolute reality is a blind urge to live and live it up more comparable to *maya* (illusory worldliness). In any case, regarding the bond between the individual and the world, Schopenhauer says:

> The terrors of death rest for the most part on the false illusion that then the I or ego vanishes, and the world remains. But rather is the opposite true, namely that the world vanishes; on the other hand, the innermost kernel of the ego endures, the bearer and producer of that subject, in whose representation alone the world had its existence. (W-II, 500)

The world does not have an independent status because it exists in the representation of man. Rather, the world is nothing but a network of representations. It seems to us that the individual entirely vanishes when his or her death occurs. In fact, the force of which the individual was a phenomenon remains. The will will be here and about in another form. But the world that individual carried in his head, will be no more. This is a curious way Schopenhauer brings home the co-foundationality of man and the world as well as the illusory nature of individuality.

WE OUGHT NOT TO BE

Schopenhauer suggests that to impart the dying man the larger teaching of death we might say to him: 'You are ceasing to be something which you would have done better never to become' (W-II, 501). In this enigmatic statement Schopenhauer tells us that the individual who had become engrossed in his individuality and, in the love of the world and all its enticements, needs to learn from death the lesson that he could have spent his life otherwise than he had. He could have denied the will rather than affirming all its dictates. Schopenhauer spells out the philosophical and moral lessons of death in the following summation of his standpoints on life and death:

> At bottom, we are something that ought not to be. Therefore, we cease to be. Egoism really consists in man's restricting all reality to his own person, in that he imagines he lives in this alone and not in others. Death teaches him something better, since it abolishes this person, so that man's true nature, that is his will, will henceforth live only in other individuals. (W-II, 507)

That 'we are something that ought not to be' seems to be a radically pessimistic statement. But there are implicit philosophical insights and moral standpoints in it. Consistent with Vedanta and Buddhism, Schopenhauer says that coming into the world (*samsara*) should not be presumed to be a happy event, for such an assumption promotes love of the world, in other words, thoughtless affirmations of the will-to-live. What distinguishes human life from all other existences is the opportunity to overcome the love of the world, to seek salvation, that is, by a denial of the will-to-live. That denial requires detachment rather than the love of the world. It is better, therefore, to begin with the assumption that mere coming into the world and being in it is not a glorious event. This does not mean that one should forthwith end one's life. It means that one should live, as far as possible, a life of detachment from the world. The same insight is contained in Socrates' statement that it is not just living but living well that counts. Schopenhauer also takes a stand against egoism. It seems to him that the greatest teaching of death is to show us how absurd egoism is. Death destroys all the pride and self-love of man in one stroke and demonstrates the unreality of egoism. It shows that a radical dualism between oneself and the others is a false assumption and so is that between oneself and the world out there. This insight is contained in the well-known saying of the Upanishads, *tat tvam asi* (that thou art).

Schopenhauer expresses his admiration for the belief in re-birth (*metempsychosis*) that prevails in Brahmanism and Buddhism, as well as among the ancient Greeks and Egyptians, and many other ancient and modern cultures. He says that metempsychosis prevails even now 'among more than half of the human race, as the firmest of convictions, with an incredibly strong practical influence'. It is Judaism and two religions springing from it, that is, Christianity and Islam that lack this belief for they assume man's creation out of nothing. Regarding reincarnation, Schopenhauer laments that 'They have succeeded, with fire and sword, in driving that consoling, primitive belief of mankind out of Europe and of a part of Asia; for how long it is uncertain' (W-II, 506). However, Christianity does have the doctrine of original sin which replaces the theory of the transmigration of souls. Schopenhauer shows his distinct preference for re-birth (*palingenesis*) over reincarnation (*metempsychosis*). *Palingenesis* is supposed to be re-birth as the result of a previous existence but appearing in a different form and with a new intellect without any recollection of the past life. Schopenhauer recognizes that this doctrine is found in 'its subtlest form' in Buddhism. Because Buddhism does not subscribe to the concept of soul, it contains a theory of re-birth without any reference to a transmigration of the soul. Thus, it regards a new birth occurring based on *karma* (deeds) of the previous birth, but appearing in a form and intellect entirely different from the past life.

Schopenhauer finds the re-birth doctrines of Hinduism and Buddhism quite logical, but he does not simply adopt their mythical forms in his own theory of after-life. He finds Buddhist *palingenesis* quite compatible with his theory that the will receives a new form and a new intellect after the death of the individual, but there is a part of the individual, namely the will, that is indestructible and lives on.

We do not come back with skin and hair, the same as we are. But we do not entirely perish or sink into nothingness. The degree to which death is regarded as an annihilation depends on how much one clings to the world and how sharp and absolute one regards the difference between oneself and the others. The loss of individuality should be regarded as the loss of a phenomenon, not of the thing-in-itself. Death also shows us that the man–world dichotomy is an artificial pre-supposition. 'From the metaphysical standpoint, the sentences "I perish but the world endures" and "the world perishes, but I endure" are not really different at bottom. . . . Death is the great opportunity no longer to be I; to him, of course, who embraces it' (W-II, 507).

Schopenhauer pays homage to the death-contemplators like Socrates, who embraced their death readily and cheerfully, having lived their life in the shadow of death, practising life-long, the detachment from excessive worldliness. They regard everything around and especially other human beings, part and parcel of their larger self, and die in the conviction that their inner being shall not perish. Such a one aims for nothing less than salvation:

> As a rule, the death of every good person is peaceful and gentle; but to die willingly, to die gladly, to die cheerfully, is the prerogative of the resigned, of him who gives up and denies the will-to-live. For he alone wishes to die actually and not apparently, and consequently needs and desires no continuance of his own person. He willingly gives up the existence that we know; what comes to him instead of it is in our eyes nothing, because our existence in reference to that one is nothing. The Buddhist faith calls that existence *nirvana*, that is to say, extinction. (W-II, 508)

CHAPTER TEN

DENIAL AND ASCETICISM

Human existence is unique in the sense that it has the possibility of knowing the overall nature of the will and acting in a way that Schopenhauer calls the denial of the will. The possibility of the will wilfully denying itself seems like a contradiction, and the turning of the will against itself will mean a forsaking of the will's essential nature. If the intuition of the thing-in-itself appears in our consciousness as will-to-live, then its complete negation or denial would seem to be an impossibility. It would amount to Being turning into nothingness or the deliberate ending of an existence. Of course, the noble and praiseworthy conduct that Schopenhauer calls the denial of the will-to-live and describes as the summit of ethical life, cannot be an absolute denial or annihilation of the will, even though his descriptions literally convey that impression. The denial of the will must mean a radical and uncommon toning down of the will's usual projects in an enlightened human existence. Schopenhauer maintains that the source of all goodness, virtue and nobility of character in man is the same as that which ultimately produces the denial of the will-to-live (W-I, 378). Thus, such a denial is qualitatively similar to a superior ethical life and conduct.

The denial of the will is a controlling of the blind will that proceeds from a holistic knowledge of the machinations of the will and of the nature of the world in which the will is omnipresent. A person who is not totally immersed in egoism and is able to see through the *principium individuationis* realizes his kinship with everything that exists around him. The whole world seems as close to him as his own person seems to the egoist. Endowed with a holistic knowledge, and overwhelmed with empathy with all living things, such a person finds the nature of this world and its sufferings unacceptable, and no longer wishes to chase the motives of his selfish projects through end-less willing. According to Schopenhauer, a sense of detachment is bound to arise in one who witnesses suffering and vain striving in the world. Thoughtfulness and compassion sublimate his egoism and incessant craving and striving for personal indulgences.

> How could he with such knowledge of the world, affirm this very life through constant acts of will . . . bond himself more and more firmly to it . . . On the other hand, that knowledge of the whole, of the inner nature of the thing-in-itself becomes the 'quieter' of all and every willing . . . Man attains to the state of voluntary renun-ciation, resignation, true composure and complete will-lessness. (W-I, 379)

What Schopenhauer seems to suggest is that it is within the range of human possibilities that the arising of a superior knowledge can enable the will to turn against itself, that is, to go against its own nature to keep on willing and striving for worldly aims and gains. Knowledge can possibly become the quieter of willing. Schopenhauer uses drastic language in describing the denial of the will as an absolute transformation from 'willing everything' to 'willing nothing at all'. As pointed out above, according to Schopenhauer's own accounts, a total annihilation of the will is not possible when one is still alive. Thus, knowledge becoming 'quieter of all and every willing' must mean for practical purposes, 'the calming down' or 'reduction of willing' to a bare minimum. The point of this denial is to 'deprive desires of their sting, close the entry to all suffering, purify and sanc-tify ourselves' (W-I, 379). 'Depriving desires of their sting' implies much like in the Buddhist sense that one must work on eliminating those desires which are cravings and obsessions that ultimately pro-duce suffering. Desires for moral good (dharma) and creativity should be cultivated. Schopenhauer's emphasis on complete renun-ciation and mortification of the flesh seems to miss the point of the middle-path stressed by the Buddha, as it also overlooks the golden mean suggested by Aristotle.

ASCETICISM AS THE HIGHEST ETHICS

Schopenhauer recognizes the difficulties in the path of a denier of the will-to-live. This state is far from being a complete transformation into a born again life. Rather, one has to constantly resist the temptations of the world and struggle to stay detached from the allurements of the will from moment to moment.

> But the illusion of the phenomenon soon ensnares us again and its motives set the will in motion once more . . . the allurements of hope, the flattery of the present, the sweetness of pleasures, the well-being that falls to the lot of our person amid the lamentations of a suffering world governed by chance and error, all these draw us back to it, and rivet the bonds anew. (W-I, 379)

The state of the denial of the will is described by Schopenhauer as 'the transition from virtue to asceticism'. The practitioner who sees through the *principium individuationis* does not merely love his neighbour, but sympathizes with and begins to have a sense of kinship to all that exists. At the same time, the realization of the toughness and misery of all existence arouses in him an aversion for the will of which he himself is to be a phenomenon. This gives him or her an impetus to live a life of utmost simplicity, voluntary poverty and asceticism. Such an ascetic practises voluntary and complete chastity, for the sexual impulse is the crux of the will-to-live. It is only the human existence that has the possibility of voluntary and complete renunciation that earns the human entity the eligibility for eventual salvation, also described as attaining to God by theistic religions. 'The rest of nature has to expect its salvation from man who is at the same time priest and sacrifice' (W-I, 381).

The ascetic renounces property and embraces voluntary poverty, not merely to offer it to the needy, but takes renunciation of ownership as an end in itself. Such a one does not want any sweets of life that may 'stir the will' or any ties that bind him to worldly business. At the same time, having given up self-love, the renunciate practises utmost humility and does not hit back at his critics and detractors. He endures 'such ignominy and suffering with inexhaustible patience and gentleness, returns good for all evil without ostentation'. The lived testimony of the saints of all noble religions points towards this real possibility of virtue culminating in asceticism. Schopenhauer indicates that this is where philosophy and religion validate each other.

> And what I have described here with feeble tongue, and only in general terms, is not some philosophical fable, invented by myself

and only of today. No, it was the enviable life of so many saints and great souls among Christians, and even more among the Hindus and Buddhists and also among the believers of other religions. Different as were the dogmas that were impressed on their faculty of reason, the inner, direct and intuitive knowledge from which alone all virtue and holiness can come, is nevertheless expressed in precisely the same way in the conduct of life. (W-I, 383)

Schopenhauer regards the saints, monks, *sadhus* and *sufis* from different religions as the prototypes of the denial of the will-to-live and holds them in high esteem for their self-abnegation. However, he maintains that his doctrine which is expressed in philosophical and abstract terms is free from myth and superstition whereas the saints and ascetics are invariably motivated by religious viewpoints of the specific sects they belong to. As far as their conduct in life goes, the ascetics of different traditions show a similar self-denial and a disregard of the worldly temptations. Schopenhauer's following remarks indicate that the difference between a saint and a philosopher is to be expected. They also seem to respond to the criticisms made by several of Schopenhauer's biographers that he did not live up to the standards of an ascetic himself.

It is therefore just as little necessary for the saint to be a philosopher as for the philosopher to be a saint; just as it is not necessary for a perfectly beautiful person to be a great sculptor, or for a great sculptor to be himself a beautiful person. In general, it is a strange demand on a moralist that he should commend no other virtue than that which he himself possesses. (W-I, 383)

On the other hand, a philosopher's life is expected to show some impact of his or her professed philosophy. Schopenhauer's philosophy is distinguished in so far as it deals with problems of existence and everyday living, although it continues to be primarily a search for truth. Schopenhauer is quite willing to use the resources of religion to explore the nature of a good and moral life. While exploring the common boundaries of philosophy and religion, Schopenhauer strives to remain non-prescriptive as he mentions in his introductory remarks to the fourth book of *WWR*: 'All philosophy is always theoretical since it is essential to it always to maintain a purely contemplative attitude, whatever to be the immediate object of investigation;

to inquire not to prescribe' (W-I, 271). Thus, in this inquiry into the rare but distinguished conduct of a select few including saints and ascetics, there must be something to admire and practise for those who are not saints themselves. When it comes to outlining the possibilities and merits of the denial of the will for all thoughtful but ordinary human beings, Schopenhauer takes things to the extreme. There seems to be no room for a middle way or moderation. The denial of the will, according to him, is a total abnegation and is essentially sparked by one's pessimism and disgust towards the way the world is an arena of suffering. The world's denial is an authentic attitude chosen by a select few who let their knowledge suppress their will as Schopenhauer quotes Spinoza: 'All that is excellent and eminent is as difficult as it is rare' (*Ethics*, V, 42).

However, it is possible to look at the example of the saints in another light and to recognize the relevance of the denial of the will for the non-saintly humanity. A simple and moderate life that rejects excessive materialism may receive its impetus from moral and contemplative goals rather than a total disgust of the world. A saint may be driven by higher spiritual truths to set up an example of an austere life so that people may find such a devoted life realistic rather than fantastic, and may emulate him or her to an extent. The saints and ascetics usually have a mission, something to teach and to inspire. They teach by example that a non-material life is very much possible and desirable.

Schopenhauer says that the philosophical doctrine of the denial of the will-to-live is visible in experience and reality in the lives of the saints and ascetics of various Western and Eastern traditions, but to learn about their lives we have to rely on inadequately written biographies and hagiographies. From the Christian tradition, he has particular regard for St Francis of Assisi, 'that true personification of asceticism and prototype of all mendicant friars', who embraced voluntary poverty and, in line with the Hindu attitude, recognized kinship with the animals. Christian mystics like Meister Eckhart are greatly admired by him. He also recommends the autobiography of Madame de Guyon 'a great and beautiful soul whose remembrance always fills me with reverence' (W-I, 385). Schopenhauer also admires the biography of Fraulein Klettenberg, penned by Goethe. In his discussion of the lives of the saintly souls, Schopenhauer abandons his usual gender bias, which was perhaps rooted in his disapproval of his mother's extravagant ways.

Schopenhauer laments that the history of the world maintains a silence about persons whose conduct was the noblest and the best, for history for the most part is a record of the affirmations and manifestations of the will in the form of power-plays, conquests, regime changes, shrewd rulers and tyrants. To recognize and celebrate the deniers of the will becomes the responsibility of philosophers for whom the life-sketches of these renunciates, badly written as they might be, are 'incomparably more important than even Plutarch and Livy'. It may be noticed that Schopenhauer places high value for philosophy contained in biographical literature. Other subsequent European thinkers including, Wilhelm Dilthey, would express similar faith in biographies as the reservoirs of lived-world-experiences (*Erlebnisse*) and as vital source-materials for philosophy.

Schopenhauer maintains that the lives of the Buddhist monks, given in the *Eastern Monarchism* by Spence Hardy, offer similar illustrations of the denial of the will as shown in the accounts of the lives of Christian saints. The same is the material of numerous biographies and religious histories (*puranas*) of the Hindu *sanyasis* (monks) and ascetics. Herein, we see that the ethics of the Hindus ordains 'love of the neighbor with complete denial of self-love, love in general not limited to the human race, but embracing all that lives' (W-I, 388). The similarities in New Testament Christianity, Hinduism and Buddhism are found to be striking by Schopenhauer. It is their suspicion of and reflection of the worldliness and their approval of renunciation that brings theistic Christianity and Hinduism and atheistic Buddhism together. This is why their saints and renunciates appear to have the same lifestyle. Schopenhauer remarks that 'we cannot sufficiently wonder at the harmony we find, when we read the life of a Christian penitent or saint and that of an Indian' (W-I, 389).

Schopenhauer warns once again that the denial of the will is not a permanent state, but its practitioner has to work on it constantly. 'We must not imagine that after the denial of the will-to-live has once appeared . . . such denial no longer waivers or falters, and we can rest on it as inherited property. It must be achieved afresh by constant struggle' (W-I, 391). Schopenhauer seems to portray the denial of the will as a matter of severe self-control or something like a constant battle with the raging will within us. In *Twilight of the Idols*, Nietzsche rejects the glamourization of the monk and speculates that moderation can be an instinctual attribute. Some people with a healthy make up and outlook may not need or want constant stimulation, that is, they may become less subjected to the will by nature. At the same time, humans being creatures of habit may not have to stifle their will when they have had sufficient practice of will-lessness, which they have freely chosen as their way of life. Thus, the saint may be a very moderate person by nature with a superior wisdom to dislike and renounce the world to the extent possible, and at the same time well-practised in giving up what people call the high life. If the doctrine of the denial of the will has to have a general following, and not just the lifestyle of a distinguished spiritual élite, Schopenhauer's extreme view of it needs modification. Of course, the saints and ascetics are the role models of a possibility that is open to all. Moderation and simplicity are options for everybody.

SUFFERING AND THE DENIAL OF THE WILL

Schopenhauer says that most people who choose the path of the denial of the will very often do so after encountering personal sufferings. A major loss or disappointment can be a catalyst for a spiritual conversion that prompts a complete resignation and ascetic life. Only a chosen few are lead by pure knowledge to practise the denial of the will. These are the persons who are greatly affected by the sufferings of the world in general and are able to see through the *principium individuationis* and be overwhelmed by universal love of mankind. They recognize in the sufferings of others their own suffering and, through a vision of their universal self, they want no better life for themselves than the lot of the bulk of suffering humanity. Whether one is converted by personal suffering and hopelessness or through empathy with the sufferings of others, the denial of the will is related to suffering and its practice involves voluntary embracing of self-denial and rejection of what the world calls the good life. This practice has been aptly called the practice or the rehearsal of death or a true philosophical life by Socrates. Schopenhauer describes such a practitioner of the will's denial as follows:

> We see him know himself and the world, change his whole nature, rise above himself and all suffering, as if purified and sanctified by it, in inviolable peace, bliss and sublimity, willingly renounce everything he formerly desired with the greatest vehemence, and gladly welcome death. (W-I, 393)

In many cases, the experience of suffering serves as a catalyst for a life of the will's denial. For some, death being near at hand and hopelessness is the cause of their renunciation. For some others, it can be a sudden misfortune or setback that leads them to realize the vanity of all endeavour. Sometimes kings, heroes and adventurers, suddenly convert to being hermits and monks. Schopenhauer cites the cases of two such conversions: Raymond Lull, who after suddenly witnessing the cancer-eaten bosom of his ladylove, gave up royalty and went on to a hermit's life; Abbe de Rance, whose youth was spent in pursuit of pleasures, suddenly stumbled against the severed head of his beloved Madame de Montebazon, later became the chief reformer of *La Trappe* monastic order in France. He revitalized this group of ascetics, whose monks are known to this day for severe austerities and utmost humility. Such examples of conversions are not confined to the previously rich and powerful, but at times even the hardened criminals, convert to a spiritual outlook while face to face with their impending execution. Schopenhauer records several so-called *gallows-sermons* delivered by such convicts shortly before their execution, remarkable for their spiritual insight (W-II, 631). These accounts were obviously culled by Schopenhauer from his daily readings of *The Times* and other English newspapers. This shows how down-to-earth and directly related to everyday life Schopenhauer's philosophy is.

Suffering contains within it a sanctifying force, according to Schopenhauer. This is because suffering makes one humble and resigns oneself to reality. 'But the sufferer . . . is worthy of reverence only when his glance has been raised from the particular to the universal, and when he regards his own suffering merely as an example of the whole . . . so that the whole of life conceived as essential suffering, thus brings him to resignation' (W-I, 396). It seems that Schopenhauer does not distinguish between having deep compassion for the sufferings of others and subscribing to the pessimistic outlook that claims that all life is suffering. While it is true that suffering is a sanctifying force that enables us to recognize that life is not a bed of roses and that the suffering of others ought to be our foremost concern, it may not and perhaps should not lead us to the extremely pessimistic view that life is a vale of tears and suffering is ineradicable. Not all saints and religious ascetics have subscribed to Schopenhauer's pessimistic world-view, according to which all sainthood and rejection of materialistic life has to be inspired by the notion that life is essentially suffering.

The Buddha certainly did not propound this simplistic viewpoint. While in the first noble truth he says that sufferings within life are real and must be the foremost concern of all thoughtful and compassionate persons, in the third noble truth he clearly maintains that *dukkha* (suffering) can be 'removed without a remainder' if the eightfold path of *dharma* (moral law), compassion and moderation are followed. Similarly, the saints of other religions are known for their cheerful disposition and their heroic resolve to help the poor, needy and downtrodden. They were not mere recluses and hermits who entirely forsake the world. Schopenhauer maintains that when a practitioner of the denial of the will rises above his personal suffering, and his grief extends beyond his narrower self and is extended to all life, then through a withdrawal of his own will he feels 'a certain loosening of his bonds, a mild foretaste of death' (W-I, 396). This indicates that denial of the will is essentially what Socrates called the practice of death, in Schopenhauer's terms, a seeing through the *principium individuationis*, a movement of knowledge beyond the principle of sufficient reason.

THE DENIAL AND THE ORIGINAL SIN

Schopenhauer's interpretation of original sin in the form of original guilt of humanity along with his concept of eternal justice has baffled many scholars of his work as well as his readers. He seems to have produced these notions by combining the Christian concept of original sin with the law of karma which is a basic doctrine of Hinduism and Buddhism. Since he regards the spirit of these religions as the same, he has no difficulty in fusing karma and original sin to come up with the notion that human beings are born laden with a guilt that is not the result of their current actions. This is perfectly understandable if we don't subscribe to the Judaic and Old Testament notion that we are God's handiwork and made out of nothing.

That man comes into the world already involved in guilt can appear absurd only to the person who regards himself as just having come from nothing, and the work of another. Hence in consequence of this guilt, which must therefore have come from his will, man rightly remains abandoned to physical and mental sufferings, even when he has practiced all these virtues, and so he is not happy. This follows from 'eternal justice' of which I spoke in Section 63 of Volume I. (W-II, 603)

It is easy to see that for us virtue is not always equal to happiness and very often bad things happen to good people. If all suffering happened due to a lack of virtue, we would just need moral good rather than salvation. But salvation has been identified as the highest goal of human life. Schopenhauer points out that Christianity, Hinduism and Buddhism proclaim this with one voice. It is clear that virtuous action is not good enough. St Paul, Augustine and Luther all maintain that 'works do not justify since we all are and remain essentially sinners' (W-II, 603). Schopenhauer emphatically says that 'original sin is really our only true sin' (W-II, 604). As these religions highlight 'we need to become something different from, indeed the very opposite of what we are . . .we need a complete transformation of our nature and disposition' (W-II, 604). Schopenhauer maintains that Hinduism, Buddhism and Christianity all teach a 'heavy guilt of the human race through existence itself', although Christianity does so indirectly, that is through the myth of the fall of man. Christianity could not be as explicit on this issue as Hinduism and Buddhism, because it had to cling to the Jewish theism and the dogma regarding creation out of nothing by the Almighty. Speaking philosophically rather than in terms of the religious myths, Schopenhauer explains why the denial of the will is necessary to properly respond to the existential guilt.

To speak without the myth, as long as our will is the same, our world cannot be other than it is. It is true that all men wish to be delivered from the state of suffering and death; they would like . . . to attain the eternal bliss . . . but not on their own feet; they would like to be carried there by the course of nature. But this is impossible; for nature is only the copy, the shadow, of our will . . . she cannot bring us anywhere except always into nature again. (W-II, 605)

Thus, according to Schopenhauer, the denial of the will is not just the attitude that saints and thinkers adopt due to their superior knowledge of the operations of the will as endless striving that is doomed to be frustrated. But it is also a proper response on their part to the nature of human condition laden with original sin (or cumulative karma). Schopenhauer draws some conclusions which can be baffling for a reader steeped in strictly European and rational thinking:

> Existence is certainly to be regarded as an error or mistake, to return from which is salvation . . . In fact, nothing else can be stated as the aim of our existence except the knowledge that it would be better for us not to exist. This, however, is the most important of all truths and must therefore be stated, however much it stands in contrast with the present day mode of European thought. (W-II, 605)

Schopenhauer's radical assertion that 'the aim of our existence (is) . . . the knowledge that it would be better for us not to exist' should be analysed in the light of its deeper meanings, implications and his sources which do not lie in 'the present day mode of European thought'. Many scholars of Schopenhauer's philosophy have dismissed such statements as confusing and illogical as well as unacceptably pessimistic. Of course, at first sight it is a pessimistic thing to say that it would have been better for us not to have come into being for this world is an unsatisfactory place to be in. It is an arena of perpetual suffering and endless striving for vain goals of the will. That is a simple rationale for Schopenhauer's pessimistic conclusions stated in the above quote. However, in order to outline the justifications for the denial of the will, he refers to the selfless lives of not only Christian but Hindu, Buddhist and Sufi saints. Now, if we ask the question regarding the rationale for the renunciation of the world by the saints and mystics, it would be both simplistic and incorrect to dismiss them as the pessimistic crowd. In the same manner, if we ask ourselves whether it is wise to dismiss all of the Eastern religions as, on the whole, pessimistic just because Schopenhauer uses a peculiar interpretation of these to revalidate his own philosophy, the answer should be in the negative. So what is the real rationale for the saints and mystics to disparage and discard the worldly ways of life? Why do Hinduism and Buddhism cast aspersions on the worldly existence (*samsara*) and uphold salvation (*nirvana*) as the highest goal of human life?

It is because these world views regard too much attachment to the worldly goals and being excessively caught up in the enticing and illusory worldliness (*maya*) as counter-productive for the spiritual growth of the human being. In order to persuade humans to go against the current of raging worldliness, they depict the world at hand (*samsara*) as inferior to salvation (*nirvana*) so that merely being in the world and loving the world does not become the highest goals of life. Those religions have created several mythological beliefs that go hand-in-hand with their philosophical viewpoint that the world must be looked at with suspicion and as something to be overcome. The belief in reincarnation depicts coming into the world cycle (*samsara*) as undesirable. This is not done because the world is utterly bad but because too much worldliness is an impediment to spiritual advancement. Thus, existence, world and worldliness are taken as challenging realities that require self-introspection, scepticism and restraint. Thus, whether the existence is assumed to be hazardous or glorious in itself depends on one's assumptions. This fundamental assumption of Hinduism and Buddhism that coming into *samsara* is undesirable was put forward to wean people away from the excessive love of the world.

However, Schopenhauer, who is already committed to the notion that the world as the arena of will's endless and hopeless striving, has found a revalidation of his pessimistic world-view in his pessimistic interpretation of Hindu and Buddhist standpoints. He downplays the optimistic accounts of those traditions regarding human life as a glorious opportunity to lead the life of *dharma* (moral law), gain knowledge of the spirit (*jnana*) and experience the bliss of love (*bhakti*) and move forward on the path to salvation (*nirvana*). Schopenhauer chooses to concentrate on the seemingly negative characterization of the world (*samsara*) in these traditions along with their theories of reincarnation and karma. In any case, his assertions such as 'it would be better for us not to exist' are based on a simplistic and pessimistic interpretation of Hindu and Buddhist doctrines which meaningfully maintain that being subject to the cycle of birth and coming back into *samsara* should not be viewed as a glorious event. Thus, the reasons behind the very first phrase in the Buddha's sermon on the four noble truths, namely, 'Birth is *dukkha* (suffering)' is much deeper than it seems. To understand it fully, we must combine it with the statement in the third noble truth, that is, '*dukkha* can be removed without a remainder,' an optimistic assertion which promotes and justifies the life of *dharma* (moral law). Schopenhauer chooses to ignore the third noble truth and focuses on the first phrase 'Birth is dukkha' which appears in the form of the statements such as 'the aim of life (is) . . . to know that it would be better for us not to exist'.

DENIAL, DETACHMENT AND ASCETICISM

True knowledge is not only an ability to see through the *principium individuationis* and gain a conviction that the same will abides in all phenomena, but also an overcoming of a delusion regarding one's separate identity and regarding meaningfulness of the will's projects. According to Schopenhauer, 'to return from this (delusion) and hence to deny its whole present endeavour is what religions describe as self-denial . . .' (W-II, 606). Schopenhauer says that the denial of the will is the pinnacle of ethics; moral virtues are merely the means of advancing self-denial or denial of the will. 'The virtuous action is a momentary passing through the point, the permanent return to which is the denial of the will-to-live' (W-II, 610). Permanent return does not mean that the denier no longer struggles and guards against the inroads of the will. It means that the self-transformation of the denier of the will is more sustained than that of one who performs sporadic acts of goodness. A practitioner of the denial is someone who accepts death as lawful and not as a catastrophe, for he or she is already well-rehearsed in voluntarily giving up what people call 'the life', that is, the life of the will. Thus, a denier of the will is not afraid of death but has a special relationship with it. Schopenhauer explains the detachment of such a one from the love of existence:

> He will be least afraid of becoming nothing in death who has recognized that he is already nothing now, and who consequently no longer takes any interest in his individual phenomenon, since in him knowledge has, so to speak, burnt up and consumed the will, so that there is no longer any will, any keen desire for individual existence, left in him. (W-II, 609)

The attachment that the worldling has with his own well-being and self-gratification is much reduced in one who denies the will, although it is hard to imagine that it can be non-existent in him, as Schopenhauer's radical statements indicate. However, having experienced a sort of voluntary death of the worldliness such a one is ready for the actual death because he neither clings to the world nor loves himself as intensely as most people do.

Schopenhauer indicates that he is aware that his philosophy will be accused of being excessively negative because it seems to end up with a negation in upholding the denial of the world as the highest ethical attitude. If philosophy is to remain connected with the problems of authentic living and coping with the suffering contained in life, in short, with actual life itself, then philosophy cannot shy away from the issues of quietism and asceticism. Schopenhauer thinks that these themes are part and parcel of metaphysics and ethics. Schopenhauer clearly believes that philosophy must pronounce on an ideal philosophical life and thereby remain relevant to life as such, including the problem of defining the nature of life as well as dealing with the problems of living and suffering. Although philosophy should not be too prescriptive, it cannot shy away from the philosophical task of outlining ethical versus the thoughtless life.

Such problems of the life-world experience should not be dismissed by philosophers just because they are also discussed in the domain of religion. Rather, religious beliefs and world-views can be analysed philosophically, so that all avenues to the issues of Being are explored through philosophical methods. While Schopenhauer explicates and admires several world-renouncing concepts of Christianity, Hinduism, Buddhism and Sufism, he filters out their mythological, ritualistic and superstitious elements, and outlines only those aspects of religious thought that elucidate the problems of metaphysics and existence that religion in the broader sense, shares with philosophy. Schopenhauer believes that all accounts of human life and Being are interesting for philosophy. In this sense, he was a precursor of contemporary European hermeneutics which defines the scope of human sciences as sciences of the spirit (*Geistwissenschaftliche*) whose subject-matter includes history, literature, religion, philosophy and other social and human sciences. Schopenhauer thinks that he is not less of a philosopher for making the leap from philosophy to a philosophical life. That leap is not only an age-old tradition in the West enriched by the likes of Socrates, Jesus and Plotinus and a series of Christian mystics, but also a time-honoured essence of the Eastern faiths. Thus, reflecting on an ideal philosophical life and on the actual lives of philosophers who lived their philosophy is part and parcel of a genuine philosophy as far as Schopenhauer is concerned.

In speaking about the philosophical and religious developments together, Schopenhauer reiterates that Christianity has the same world-renouncing spirit that Brahmanism and Buddhism possess. According to him, Christianity, although formally connected with Judaism and the Old Testament, is different in spirit from both Judaism and Islam. It also carries in it a radical departure from ancient Greek thought, which is preoccupied with the cosmos, and despite the reorientation of the philosophical enterprise towards the study of the soul introduced by Socrates, remains dominantly world oriented. Greek and Roman thought remains cosmocentric, and Christianity alone taught them to 'look beyond the narrow, paltry, and ephemeral life on earth, and no longer to regard that as an end in itself' (W-II, 627). Regarding the most important issue in philosophy, namely, the necessity to rise above the worldly-mindedness and to embrace truly philosophical life, namely a life of asceticism, the ancient Greek philosophy is certainly deficient. 'Although the ancients were far advanced in almost everything else, they had remained children in the principal matter . . . the fact that one or two philosophers, Pythagoras and Plato, taught otherwise, alters nothing as regards the whole' (W-II, 628).

Thus, Christianity presented a fundamental truth which is the same as it appears in Hinduism and Buddhism, namely, the need for salvation from an imperfect world, attainable through renunciation, otherwise known as the denial of the will. This denial involves going against nature or the matter-of-course worldly ways. But this practice is both difficult and against the natural tendency of mankind, Schopenhauer acknowledges. The motives of those who follow this path remain abstract and inaccessible to most people. Thus, religions sought the aid of mythology to bring home this truth to the masses. Hence, they present the picture on a larger canvass through the myths such as the fall of man and reincarnation, etc. However, philosophy must approach this issue directly in terms of abstract concepts. Thus, philosophy being free of myth and symbolism is related to religion 'as a straight line is to several curves running near it'. Philosophy makes it clear that true freedom for the human being has to do with the ability of the will to affirm or deny. Thus, denial of the will can be the experience of the highest freedom if it is not a mere mortification, but a freely chosen way of life.

IS DENIAL OF THE WILL POSSIBLE?

Is denial of the will a realistic possibility even for a saint? Since Schopenhauer devotes a sizable portion of his work to this theme and regards this concept as the finest achievement of his philosophy, he must be seriously recommending this practice for all thoughtful persons. Is there a contradiction between Schopenhauer's assertion that the will is ever-present and omnipresent and that it can possibly be denied or eliminated? If human being is will through and through and if it is the very thing-in-itself, then how can an existing human being deny the core of his existence? The denial as such seems to be an act of will too. But it is an act of the will to abolish itself. We will have to acknowledge that an absolute denial of the will is impossible for a person still alive. He or she cannot stop willing altogether while in a body. Thus, the denial of the will must mean practice of restraint and willing only for the purposes of existing and serving higher goals of benevolence and compassion. It must be a turning away from intense cravings of a selfish nature to positive goals of an altruistic kind. It must be a decision of the will to transform itself from a mode of stronger willing to a weaker willing. It must be a self-restraint of the will, not the self-annihilation of the will. At the same time, the practice itself must be subject to stronger or moderate degrees. The denial of a saint is much stronger and serves as an example for thoughtful persons to imbibe the self-restraint of the saint in their lives to the extent possible in their worldly existence. It is the same as to say suicide is not warranted for one who practises death or contemplates death in the acts of living. Although Schopenhauer's statements regarding the denial of the will appear to be too radical and hinting towards the possibility of the slow killing of the will, he does not do so at the cost of compromising the indestructibility of the will which he compares to the indestructibility of matter.

What are the gains or aftermath of the practice of the denial of the will-to-live. Schopenhauer suggests that the gains or the rewards of such a denial cannot be described in terms of the worldly reality. It is often said that one gets nothing or sheer freedom from everything. Schopenhauer explains it as follows. 'My teaching . . . can speak here only of what is denied or given up; but what is gained in place of this, what is laid hold of, it is forced to describe as nothing . . . yet it still does not follow from this that it is nothing absolutely' (W-II, 612).

Schopenhauer seems to suggest that a superior knowledge that prompts one to practice self-denial is not altogether profitless. It gives one tranquility and relief from suffering involved in chasing the will's inexhaustible aims. At the same time, this peace of mind is the result of a knowledge of one's kinship with all that exists and especially with all living things. This feeling appears after the giving up of all obsessions with one's narrower self or a false sense of individuality, and experiencing a freedom from *principium individuationis*. One gains an insight that one possesses a larger death-less self and the feeling of deathlessness has to be a liberating experience.

Some critics have pointed out that while Schopenhauer speaks like a Vedantist here, outpouring the gains of his readings of the Upanishads, he seems to amalgamate the Vedic Hindu world-view with Buddhism. Not only that, he also asserts that Christianity upholds the same viewpoint regarding the spiritual possibilities of self-denial. He finds it curious that there is hardly any difference in the lifestyles and spiritual insights of Christian, Hindu, Buddhist and Sufi ascetics. It is amazing that these mystics and saints, who had little or no knowledge of each other, even within the same tradition, would arrive at remarkably similar conclusions regarding the nature of things. Schopenhauer quotes the Christian mystic, Madame de Guyon in her wonderful biography *Les Torrens*, remarking that 'in true love there is no sense of I or me or mine.' This is what a Hindu mystic experiencing the vision of *Brahman* would say; this is what Tamil Bhakti saints of South India say in the *Kural*. The Hindu Vedanta tradition places a high value on getting rid of mine-ness (*mamta*) and self-love (*moha*). Schopenhauer also quotes the Buddha as saying 'my disciples, reject the idea that I am this or this is mine' (W-II, 614). He also calls the life of St Francis of Assisi as a '*sanyasi* existence', that is, the typical existence of a homeless Hindu monk. It is amazing that St Francis has the same regard and love for animals that the Hindus are conjoined to have by their scriptures. St Francis calls animals his sisters and brothers consistent with Hindu and Buddhist beliefs (W.II, 614).

But those with a scholarly bent of mind will frown upon Schopenhauer's amalgamation of the saints of Christianity, Hinduism and Buddhism. How could these actively religious faithful abandon their distinct dogmas and pre-suppositions? How could the state of mind of a Hindu mystic who believes in the identity of the personal self (*atman*) with the universal self (*brahman*) be the same as a Buddhist saint (*arhat*) who got rid of the notion that there exists anything like self (*atman*), and who has little to do with God? How could these Eastern religions be similar to Christianity for which existence of God is all important? While Schopenhauer acknowledges that such doctrinal distinctions do exist and matter a lot to the believers of these religions, the other-worldly spirit and the view of the current lifespan as not being all in all for the human entity is what brings these traditions together. They also teach overcoming of self-love and practice of the love of the neighbours, compassion and nonviolence the same way. No wonder then, despite their doctrinal differences, they produce a large number of renunciates indistinguishable from each other in their asceticism and spiritual outlooks. The denial of the will-to-live is at the summit of Schopenhauer's philosophical achievement and through a secularization and universalization of the examples from religion he has attempted to bridge the gap between philosophy and philosophical life.

NOTES

CHAPTER THREE: THE WORLD AS WILL

[1] Martin Heidegger, 'The Thinker as Poet' in A. Hofstadter, ed. and trans. *Poetry, Language, Thought* (New York: Harper & Row, 1971), p. 4.

[2] For a thinker that thought is the inspiration and the goal, the point of departure and the endpoint of his thinking.

CHAPTER FIVE: AESTHETICS AND THE ARTS

[1] M. Hiriyanna, *Art Experience* (Mysore: Kavyalaya Publishers, 1954), p. 27.

[2] Martin Heidegger, 'The Origin of the Work of Art' in A. Hofstadter, ed. and trans. *Poetry, Language, Thought* (New York: Harper and Row, 1971), pp. 15–87.

[3] Heidegger, 'The Origin of the Work of Art', pp. 15–87.

[4] Hiriyanna, *Art Experience*, pp. 2, 7.

CHAPTER SEVEN: A WELCOME TO EASTERN THOUGHT

[1] Michael Fox, 'Schopenhauer on Death, Suicide and Self-renunciation', in Michael Fox, ed., *Schopenhauer: His Philosophical Achievement* (New York: Barnes and Noble Books, 1980), p. 161.

[2] David Cartwright, 'Schopenhauer on Suffering, Death, Guilt and the Consolation of Metaphysics', in Bric von der Luft, ed., *Schopenhauer: New Essays in Honour of his 200th Birthday* (Lewiston, NY: Edwin Mellon Press, 1988).

[3] Bryan Magee, *The Philosophy of Schopenhauer* (Oxford: Clarendon Press, 1997), pp. 13, 260.

[4] From *Samyutta-nikaya*, in S. Radhakrishnan and C. A. Moore, ed. *A Sourcebook in Indian Philosophy* (Princeton, NJ: Princeton University Press, 1973), p. 274.

[5] Ibid., p. 289.
[6] Ibid., p. 274.
[7] Ibid., p. 274.
[8] Ibid., p. 274.

SUGGESTIONS FOR FURTHER READING

SCHOPENHAUER'S WORKS

Schopenhauer's writings are lucid, free of scholarly quibbles and adorned by classical citations. The power of his writing shines even through a translation. That makes him an exceptionally accessible philosopher for scholarly as well as general readers. Although there is still a need for scholarly analyses of his system, his concepts and his sources, the reading of his original works remains indispensable for serious students of his philosophy.

The World as Will and Representation, Volumes I and II, trans. E. F. J. Payne. New York: Dover Publications, 1966.
The Fourfold Root of the Principle of Sufficient Reason, trans. E. F. J. Payne. La Salle, IL: Open Court Publishing Company, 1974.
Parerga and Paralipomena: Short Philosophical Essays, trans. E. F. J. Payne. Oxford: Clarendon Press, 1974.
Essay on the Freedom of the Will, trans. Konstantin Kolenda. New York: The Bobbs- Merrill Company, 1960.
On the Basis of Morality, trans. E. F. J. Payne. New York: The Bobbs-Merrill Company, 1965.
Manuscript Remains in 4 Volumes, ed. Arthur Hübscher, trans. E. F. J. Payne. New York: Berg, 1988.
On the Will in Nature, trans. E. F. J. Payne. New York: Berg, 1992.

LIFE AND TIMES OF SCHOPENHAUER

Safranski, Rüdiger, *Schopenhauer and the Wild Years of Philosophy*, trans. Edward Osers. Cambridge, MA: Harvard University Press, 1990.
Wallace, W., *Life of Schopenhauer*. London: Walter Scott, 1890.

Zimmern, H., *Schopenhauer: His Life and His Philosophy*. London: Longmans, Green & Co., 1876.

WORKS ON SCHOPENHAUER

Atwell, John, *Schopenhauer: The Human Character*. Philadelphia: Temple University Press, 1990.

Barua, Arati, ed., *Schopenhauer and Indian Philosophy*. New Delhi: Northern Book Centre, 2008.

Berger, Douglas L., *The Veil of Maya: Schopenhauer's System and Early Indian Thought*. Binghamton, NY: Global Academic Publishing, 2008.

Copleston, Frederick, *Arthur Schopenhauer: Philosopher of Pessimism*. London: Barnes & Noble, 1975.

Halbfass, Wilhelm, *India and Europe: An Essay in Understanding*. Albany, NY: State University of New York Press, 1988.

Hamlyn, D. W., *Schopenhauer: The Arguments of the Philosophers*. London: Routledge & Kegan Paul, 1980.

Hannan, Barbara, *The Riddle of the World: A Reconsideration of Schopenhauer's Philosophy*. Oxford: Oxford University Press, 2009.

Jacquette, Dale, *The Philosophy of Schopenhauer*. Montreal: McGill Queen's University Press, 2005.

Janaway, Christopher, ed., *The Cambridge Companion to Schopenhauer*. Cambridge: Cambridge University Press, 1999.

Magee, Bryan, *The Philosophy of Schopenhauer*. Oxford: Clarendon Press, 1983.

Singh, R. Raj, *Death, Contemplation and Schopenhauer*. Aldershot, Hampshire, UK: Ashgate Publishing Ltd., 2007.

Wicks, Robert, *Schopenhauer*. Malden, MA: Blackwell Publishing, 2008.

Young, Julian, *Schopenhauer*. New York: Routledge, 2005.

INDEX

CPSIA information can be obtained
at www.ICGtesting.com
Printed in the USA
LVHW011723290921
699005LV00008BA/338